NARROW GAUGE AT WAR 3

THE

LIGHT TRACK FROM ARRAS

*A descriptive account of the activities
of the 19th & 31st Light Railway Companies,
Royal Engineers during the World War*

ISBN 1 871980 40 2

Printed by
Postprint, Taverner House, Harling Road, East Harling
Norwich NR16 2QR

Published by
Plateway Press, Taverner House, Harling Road, East Harling
Norwich NR16 2QR

Contents

Page

Preface iv

Historical Background ix

Foreword xii

Introduction xiv

Chapter One: The Formation of the 31st 1

Chapter Two: "Q" Dump 9

Chapter Three: Operating 16

Chapter Four: Tales of the Trains 29

Chapter Five: The German Offensive, March, 1918 38

Chapter Six: The Turn of the Tide 45

Introduction to Chapter Seven 58

Chapter Seven: The 19th Company 60

Chapter Eight: Apres la Guerre 68

Appendix One: Details of Track and Rolling Stock 70

Appendix Two: List of Officers, NCOs and Men of the 31st Company 74

Appendix Three: List of Officers, NCOs and Men of the 19th Company 76

Appendix Four: Tractor Crews, Marcoing 78

Diagram of Duty Board 79

Diagram of Meal Indicator 79

Preface

by Keith Taylorson

"The Light Track from Arras" was published in 1931 under the imprint of "The Heathfield Press" of London SE7. It is one of only three[1] published accounts of day to day life in the Light Railway Operating Companies of the War Department Light Railways known to exist, and, of the three, is by far the longest. It is thus an extremely valuable document, rendered even more so by its very limited print run; in a footnote to the first edition, the author records how its production had taken up seven months of his spare time, and was printed on a 'small hand machine.' It was only with the co-operation of his printer (an ex Royal Engineer), who made materials available at cost, that the book was ever published at all. Today only a handful of copies survive.

Most readers will, I hope, have at least an outline knowledge of the history of the War Department Light Railways (WDLR). Forged in the crucible of the most savage war ever to ravage this – or any other – century, the network of 60cm gauge lines was conceived, designed and constructed in a matter of months – virtually overnight in railway terms – to resolve the crisis in supply of ammunition to the front lines of the British and Dominion

One of the first railways operated by the WDLR was an ex French Army system at Saulty-l'Arbret, south-west of Arras. Also inherited from the French were the Kerr Stuart 0-6-0T and Decauville wagons seen in this September 1916 view. *(Jim Peden collection)*

Prior to the development of the War Department Light Railways, most transport of supplies and ammunition to the front lines was by horse power. 'Corduroy' roads like this kept the supply lines open in good weather, but after heavy rain these too became virtually impassable. *(Australian 'official' photo)*

forces in France and Belgium. The British Army's ability to conduct offensives was being compromised by the unreliability of ammunition supply, in a campaign increasingly decided by the volume and intensity of artillery fire that could be brought to bear before an attack. When road transport failed, the War Department officially sanctioned the use of 60cm gauge light railways, and these grew from small beginnings to eventually total 834 miles of track on the Western Front alone.

The full story of the WDLR's development, operation, and motive power is recounted in W. J. K. Davies definitive book *"Light Railways of the First World War"* (D&C 1964) and my own more modest accounts *"Narrow Gauge at War"* and *"Narrow Gauge at War 2"* (Plateway Press, 1987 and 1996). All three books deliberately focused on the technical and factual aspects of the WDLR's story, and there was little scope for introducing anecdotal information or of naming individuals. Any author recounting the story of the WDLR has to keep in mind that the railway troops – some of them volunteers, but mostly conscripts – had to endure conditions of extreme privation and danger – artillery fire is no respecter of 'rear echelon' status – and many died or were injured in the course of their duties.

Having said this, it has to be recognised that every war in history has another side to it. Men are thrown together in an alien environment in which comradeship, and the art of

Traction engines were used as well, but were also vulnerable to muddy conditions. This John Fowler (Leeds) engine has come to grief while towing a 6-inch gun near Feuchy, east of Arras, in May 1917.

(Imperial War Museum Q5254)

working together, become not just desirable, but necessary mechanisms for survival. Friendships of a most intimate nature are formed, and the military unit (be it Platoon, Squad, Battalion or – in this context – Light Railway Operating Company) becomes, for the duration, a substitute for family. It is not surprising therefore that even in the most arduous of conditions, soldiers can enjoy their work, revel in the opportunities that military life provides, and take refuge in whatever humour can be extracted from the grim realities of everyday life. Indeed it is this last feature which must have prevented many soldiers from 'cracking up' in a world which seemed at the time (and indeed still now looks) to have gone completely insane.

It is no contradiction, therefore, that much of Heritage's text has a light-hearted tone, and highlights the 'positive' side of life in a well-organised and highly motivated military unit. As he records, many of the WDLR staff were drawn from the ranks of the main line railway companies, the LROC's having been originally created by a 'comb-out' of men in the ranks with railway experience. Railway employees were used to working together, solving problems and making the best use of equipment and manpower ... skills that were put to the test as never before in the primitive conditions of the Western Front. Only a handful of the WDLR troops can have had experience of laying lightweight temporary track, of rerailing

The darker side of trench life: German prisoners of war act as stretcher bearers and carry an injured British soldier to safety.
(collection – Keith Taylorson)

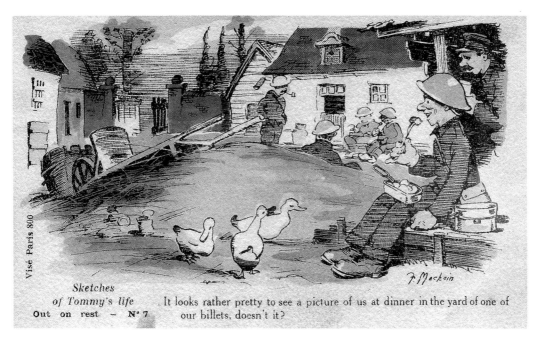

The lighter side: this artist-drawn card in the "sketches of Tommy's life" series published in Paris shows a precious moment of relaxation in a rear area.
(collection – Keith Taylorson)

locomotives and wagons virtually on a daily basis, and of operating and maintaining the then revolutionary petrol locomotives. How these skills were quickly and cheerfully learned, and passed on to newcomers to the Companies, is the central theme of Heritage's text ... along with the vicissitudes of 'trench' life, the frustrations this engendered, and the sense of achievement attained when the job was done.

"The Light Track from Arras" is an extremely important, as well as highly readable, work, and only by studying it can present-day readers gain a real appreciation of the magnificent achievements of the soldier/railwaymen, who exchanged secure and safe work at home for the dangers of life at the Front, and in doing so played a vital part in the ultimate Allied victory.

Brighton,
September 1998

[1] The *"Railway Gazette"* Special War Transportation Number, September 21, 1920.
[2] An account by Arthur Stead published in *"The Locomotive"* magazine, September 14, 1946.

EDITOR'S NOTE

In order to maintain the 'flavour' of the original text, no attempt has been made to correct the occasional minor error made by the author, eg reference to the Simplex locomotives as 'PE's (they were of course 4wPM's). However to avoid any present day reader being mislead, it should be noted that the author's reference on page 73 to ex WDLR locomotives being used on the Lynton and Barnstaple Railway is incorrect. Although the L&B was constructed to the same gauge as the WDLR, all its equipment was purpose built.

K. T.

Historical Background

The initial German offensive of 1914 took the Kaiser's armies deep into France and Belgium and ensured that the next four years of the war (with its resultant devastation to land and property) took place on the Allies' territory. However the offensive failed to win two key objectives – capture of Paris in the centre, or of the French channel ports in the north. By 1916, the front had stabilised to a line running from a point between Dunkerque and Oostende, southwards to Reims and Verdun, with Ypres, Armentières, Arras and Albert remaining in Allied hands. These and other towns, although insignificant in military or industrial terms, became nodal points around which fighting was to rage for the following two years.[1]

Until 1916 the area around Arras was held by the French Tenth Army. Although the town remained in Allied hands the German armies were for a long period only a few miles away and their heavy artillery was able to pound it with impunity. Many important buildings were destroyed and much of the housing made uninhabitable.

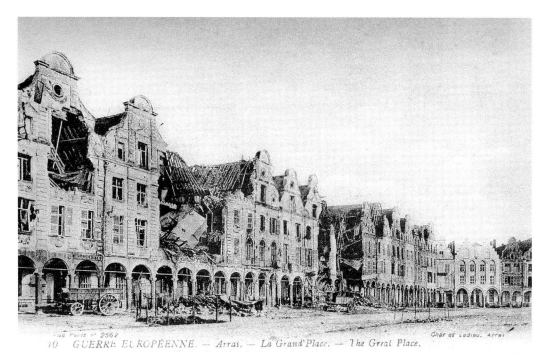

10   *GUERRE EUROPÉENNE. — Arras. — La Grand'Place. — The Great Place.*

Severe damage was caused to Arras by German shellfire in the early days of the War. This is Grand Place, the heart of the old town.   *(collection – Keith Taylorson)*

Tanks were used by the British Army in the later stages of the battles of Arras. IRON DUKE rumbles majestically through the shattered streets of the town on 10th April 1917.

(Imperial War Museum Q6418)

In 1916, as a result of the catastrophic losses to the French Army caused by the German offensive at Verdun, the British Third Army took over this sector, as part of an Allied effort to relieve pressure on the increasingly exhausted French. The disastrous Somme offensive, resulting in thousands of British deaths, took place in the area to the south of Arras. It was the failure of this offensive to achieve its main objectives (blamed in part on deficiencies in ammunition supply) that led directly to the creation of the War Department Light Railways, and the beginning of the huge network of 2ft gauge light railways around Arras that are the subject of Heritage's narrative.[2]

On April 9th 1917 the British Armies embarked on a major offensive centred on Arras, aimed at eliminating a German-held bulge between the town and the objectives gained further south on the Somme. The attacks were preceded by a 48-hour artillery bombardment in which 2,879 guns (989 of them 'heavy') were deployed – one every nine yards. This time, thanks to the efficiency of the supply operation, there was no shortage of ammunition. The new British gas shells were particularly successful in neutralising the German artillery, and killing off their draught horses. British, Canadian and Australian troops all took part in the offensive, which while failing to make a decisive breakthrough, succeeded in advancing the

Allied front line up to four miles, the recapture of Fampoux and Monchy le Preux, and the taking of 13,000 German prisoners. The light railways were kept at full stretch during this period bringing up ammunition and troop reserves, and taking back the inevitable casualties. Construction of light railways into newly captured areas, and repairs to existing lines, were a constant task.

Although steady pressure was kept up on the Germans, there was to be no significant gain in territory by the Allies in the next 12 months. Indeed it was the Germans who – with increased strength in the West following the Russians' collapse on the Eastern front – were to make the largest gains. On March 21st 1918 the German Second, Seventeenth and Eighteenth Armies (63 divisions in all) launched a massive attack on a broad front from Vimy Ridge southwards through Cambrai and St Quentin. The offensive broke through completely south of the Somme, but was held at Arras, despite a further strong attack on March 28th.[3] The offensive, although beaten back eventually by the Allies – helped by the influx of fresh American manpower – caused great alarm to the British commanders, and massive amounts of light railway material were destroyed, either by enemy action, or by the WDLR troops themselves to avoid its capture by the Germans. Heritage's narrative well captures the frenzied atmosphere of this traumatic time, when it seemed that the Germans might after all succeed where they had failed in 1914.

However, the March 1918 offensive was the German Armies' last throw. Exhausted politically and economically (although still strong militarily) Germany was unable to withstand the renewed Allied offensives in 1918, and sued for peace in November 1918. The Light Railway Operating Companies were 'stood down', though a number of railways remained in use on reconstruction work right into the early 1920's.

[1] See the maps in NARROW GAUGE AT WAR (p4) and NARROW GAUGE AT WAR 2 (p10) for more details of the position of the front line in 1916 and 1918.

[2] See NARROW GAUGE AT WAR 2 Chapter 1 for more information on the development and organisation of the WDLR.

[3] For a full account of the Arras campaigns see Liddell Hart's A HISTORY OF THE FIRST WORLD WAR Chapters 7 and 8. The distinguished military historian describes Arras as "the actual rock on which their (the Germans') plan broke."

Foreword

In presenting this book I should like to point out I have no literary aspirations. This is the first book I have ever written and no doubt it will be the last. So in view of these remarks I would like to offer excuses which are due for any shortcomings that may be contained herein. My object in writing it has been to provide a lasting souvenir of the days we spent together during the War with the 19th and 31st Companies; something we can take out of the bookcase or from a drawer and look at, and fetch back old memories. In the absence of any authentic data I have had to rely on memory and whilst it was my intention originally to write a more or less formal history of the two Companies, I decided to record my own experiences in the main and introduce places, events and times; and by doing this would assist those readers who were members of the respective companies to recall their own adventures. The facts relating to the 19th Company, apart from their good service with the 31st, have been written by Mr W. Hill, and gaps I have not been able to fill owing to my being absent from the Company in March, 1918, have been covered with the assistance of Sgt. G. Rattray, whom I have to thank in consequence. It was also my intention to give a list of the entire Personnel of the two Companies, but having written to R.E. Records, Chatham, and War Records, Isleworth, without their being able to assist, I have only been able to quote from memory and from details given by the above but it is intended to issue a "slip-in" supplement in the future as information comes to hand.

I have, as far as possible, kept out names of persons in the descriptive portion, but I hope no offence will be taken by those whose names do appear, as none is meant, and that the remarks will be treated in a broad spirit. There is always a penalty in being famous and I find this out on Re-Union nights when offered more refreshments than I can manage, being just over the border line and a teetotaller normally.

Possibly some of the ladies may be curious as to what we did get up to in France during the War and may read this book. To these it will recall the days of air-raids, sugar and meat rations, and potato queues. It will recall those dainty little cushion covers with *"Souvenir d'Arras"* which we sent home and which were very nice to look at but did not always fit in with the scheme of furnishing. It will recall the silk cards which we sent with *"Je pense à vous"* worked thereon; the Green Letters we sent, wherein we wrote the nice things which we were too bashful to put in open letters for Capt. Burge, Mr Cannon and the other officers to read. It will recall to them those golden moments of Leave, when we came out of the Fog of Mystery and when our experience was of one unreal pleasant dream, from which we expected to awake any minute.

To those of the younger generation who may glance at my effort, I would say, these were the days of Adventures both ghastly and glorious. We do not wish them again in spite of their bright side and we wish them to be spared from them. "Peace, and Goodwill to all men" should be their motto for the future. There is honour and glory to be won in the fields of industry; let us hope they will be spared the futile efforts of War.

To those who served with the Companies I would ask that in the event of circumstances preventing them attending the Re-union they will get out this book the last week in February and glance through it and recall old comrades. Possibly this book may reach some who cannot attend the Re-union at all. From those I shall be pleased to read greetings to the assembly, and I will be pleased to hear from them at any time.

It is felt that a few words of comment must be recorded in conclusion. A friend with a little experience in the publishing world, when asked for his opinion after having read the MS., said it was something out of the ordinary as regards War books. This could be taken in two ways – probably it will. He assured me, however, it was pretty good. This may have been encouragement to a novice; for myself, it could have been better or again, even worse – this the reader must decide. Its preparation has given me great pleasure – and also an idea of the difficulties met with by authors, printers and publishers. The cost of production through the usual channels would have been at least 11s. per copy, and it is only by the co-operation of the printer, Mr W. Chas. Boucher, that its production has been possible. It has taken most of his spare time for over seven months, and although anxious to help, my services have naturally been restricted by the highly skilled and technical nature of the work. The press used, being a small hand machine, had limitations, and many obstacles had to be surmounted.

Therefore I must record my thanks and appreciation of his services, and for producing the work at the cost price of materials, which it is hoped the sales will cover. Being an ex-R.E. (No. 7 Army Troops Company), sentiment has given him the interest necessary for the completion of the work, and we both hope its reading has given pleasure. If so, we shall have gained our reward.

T. Heritage,
5 First Avenue, Bromley, Kent

Introduction

by Capt. W. S. BURGE
(O.C. 31st L.R.O. Co. R.E.)

What does one remember, after 16 years, of those amateur soldiering days when we broke off for a spell from the little life and took our chance in a good adventure? Looking back, we are able in places to see the woods without the trees, whereas in the confusion of those years few of us outside the General Staff were able to see the woods for trees, and didn't this apply to the P.B.I., particularly in places like High Wood, Delville Wood, Maple Copse?

In speaking of this Light Railway Company, it is only right we should acknowledge first the Infantry who were, in fact, the hub around which we all revolved, for the whole function of the Light Railway Companies was to fetch and carry for the Infantry and Artillery. Our job was good, safe and easy compared with that of the Infantry and Gunners.

Where was it we first met? I see it in my mind's eye though the name is gone; anyway, it was just north of Arras and I had been told to go there and find a certain Officer named Webster, and then wait till an indefinite number of men turned up from various parts of the British Front who in turn would seem as if they were looking for an Officer.

Of course, it was night and raining as usual, but I did in fact find Webster, and a great concourse of men up and down the lines from various other Units. Webster's first question was, "Are we going to drive mules or locomotives?". Because he had had some months recently in the company of mules

Materials for trench construction and maintenance were a major traffic on the light railways. Here, duck boards (to form flooring for waterlogged trenches) are loaded onto a 2ft gauge trolley at a Royal Engineers dump near Arras, before being transported by light railway to the front line area.

(Imperial War Museum Q2664)

and he was getting really fond of them – he knew a trick that would make a mule run backwards up a hill and deliver a truck of ammo to the right battery when in full action in the dark. Unfortunately, mules were going to be a thing of the past and it was for that very object we were being formed.

There followed several days of sorting out – days in which from morning till night we played the game of questioning.

One of the first questions I asked was from my headquarters – "Was it really true that this 31st L.R.O. Co. was to have enough sergeants, sergeant majors and other exalted ranks to stock a Battalion; and if so, why?" Answer, "Yes" – and the reason was that these Railway Companies were to be highly technical and top heavy with brains. It very soon became evident that we had, in fact, a really wonderful collection of men nearly all of whom were recruited from one branch or other of the British Railways, and the difficulty was to know which of these 200 odd men were not fitted for exalted ranks.

And so started an R.E. Company that to this day I have always believed was not equalled for its own peculiar work anywhere on the British Front.

There was some fun in getting our mechanical equipments – I think the correct word should be "strength", shouldn't it? Anyhow, we didn't quite know whether steam, petrol or petrol-electric locos would be most useful, but a Canadian Company not far away who were debating the same question decided that our petrol locos would be more useful than their steamers, with the result that one morning we found some nine broken-down steam locos, occupying the sidings where the evening before had been about twelve newly repaired petrol tractors. I complained to my Canadian Colonel and although he was a great poker player, he for once looked quite embarrassed. He must have used some influence, persuasion or force, for very soon after this a strange Canadian turned up with our petrol tractors and took back the steam locos.

Detail becomes blurred after sixteen years, but what do I see that still stands out as representing an achievement worth placing on record?

Before this Company was started, everything on the 17th Corps Front was taken up to the lines and guns by either horses, mules, road transport or by carrying parties. Men, mules and transport were bogged in the mud night after night: guns were left without ammo, men without rations; and the more the roads and trenches were used the worse these conditions became.

When the 31st L.R.O. Co. got organised they built a Control Room at "Q" Dump, Arras, and from this our little 60cm. trains were conducted and piloted up the lines to the guns and trenches each night. In this Control Room telephone contact was maintained with our single loop control posts and every train on the lines was shown on the control diagram. Breakdown vans were equipped and teams of men, trained in the gentle art of lifting a loco out of a shell-hole in thirty minutes with not even a sky-hook to pull from, were sent out at a moment's notice wherever needed.

During the day the traffic for the night was organised, and after dusk up it went in a swarm of small trains, sometimes in convoys, sometimes in single truck units. They had no lights, no signals, but just crept out on crazy little rails weighing only 15lbs per yard and with a gauge of only 60cm (about 2 feet). On this line, laid mostly on mud and light metal sleepers, our little army of trains set forth at an average speed of six to eight miles per hour with ten tons of ammo or material in each truck. The speed sounds slow, but what about that weight on those lines? Every tractor driver and guard when they set out went on a very real adventure with no body of men to "carry them through" – they were launched on their own with the full knowledge that anything might happen at any moment, but whatever did happen they nearly always delivered the goods one way or other.

And in total, what did this amount to at the height of the Company's activities? My memory is that for months they averaged 1,100 to 1,200 tons of materials delivered per night, and on occasions 1,500 tons. This means that between 100 and 150 trains with their pairs of men got through their job each night. Knowing the conditions under which they worked, I think this was a very wonderful performance.

And what happened to the roads? They were relieved of all this traffic, for the 31st Company did its job. It was a difficult job well done under difficult conditions that called for individual pluck and

Although not designed for conveying troops, the light railways were often used for this in rear areas. This view of a party of Canadian troops returning from Divisional baths graphically illustrates the carrying capacity of a 2ft gauge train.   *(Canadian 'official' photo).*

resource without the inspiration of attack or battle conditions. How did Cannon and his small band of men get the "stuff" out from the main line station day after day while the Boche were paying special attention to the railhead with their naval gun from, I believe, Douai?

How was it that the guns in Battery Valley, after first being starved for ammo when they had to rely on road transport and carrying parties, were finally glutted with it after the 31st Company had got going?

How was it that in our attack that started early in April – I believe the 4th, in a blinding snow-storm our guns had more than sufficient ammo to blot out the enemy batteries? Well, these things were the result of individual pluck and endeavour, bound together with a wonderful team spirit and pride in the Company.

I do not think civil life can ever cultivate these things to the same extent, and those of us who served with the Company have something to be thankful for.

Chapter One

The Formation of the 31st

"Particulars of NCOs and men required with experience of railway operating and railway workshops, and in the following trades. etc., etc."

Thus read the Orderly Room Sergeant of the 24th London Regiment "The Queen's". "Here's a posh job for some of the Boys," he remarked to the Post Orderly's Assistant. "Don't you wish it was you?".

"Well, I was employed on the railway in peace time," came the reply, "but it will be the usual stunt. Hand in your name and particulars and hear no more about it. We've heard that yarn before. I've seen chaps caught with "Who can ride a bicycle?" and they get detailed to clean the dixies in the cook-house".

But the Doubting Thomas chanced it and two months later found him with mixed feelings "stepping" the sleepers of the R.O.D. Spur from Dickebusch to Reninghurst in the Ypres Salient, with a movement order to report to the Transportation Depot, Boulogne. Halting a moment, he turned back and gave a last look at the transport lines of his old Regiment, with a pang of regret recalling all the old faces he was leaving – some, but only too few, of the old originals who had landed with the Battalion – and wishing they were coming with him. Resuming his journey, he speculated on the future. "They're going to make a new railway from Dieppe to Poperinghe," he had been informed by the Regimental Orderly Room Rumourist, "and that's what they want you chaps for. Well, I've had my share of the line." he ruminated.

After a repast of *oeufs, chips, cafe and pain du beurre* at Ouderdom, a passing lorry was hailed and Poperinghe was reached. After a wait of several hours, which was well spent in viewing the shops in the town and Talbot House, our friend joined the leave train en route to Boulogne and the future. Thus the 31st was formed and at the same time as our friend made the journey, NCOs and men from all parts of France and Belgium were passing through the same experience, to meet in Boulogne to form one of the finest Companies that ever wore the R.E. Badge.

The journey to Boulogne was of the usual leisurely nature in the "sleeping cars" prevailing at the period "*8 chevaux, 40 hommes*", Machonochies and Fray Bentos being the dining car fare and the loco driver doling out tepid water grudgingly from the ejector to make the inevitable "drum up". Finally, Boulogne was reached, the lucky ones making for the quay and the nearly as lucky being directed to Marlboro Lines Camp. After the formalities of the Reception Committee had been disposed of, the Orderly Sergeant conducted the new arrivals to tents for a subsequent sorting out.

Every train running into Boulogne brought in parties who marched up the hill into the Camp to swell the numbers, and the size of the Camp grew rapidly. Things were very

The author's journey to join his unit was on board a train of the ubiquitous French railways 4-wheel vans designed to carry '8 horses or 40 men.' This trainload of troops going up to Mount St Eloi may well exceed the permitted loading. *(Imperial War Museum Q327)*

leisurely for its occupants and the life came as a welcome relief to almost everyone. Except for the usual camp fatigues (which the wily ones managed to dodge) no drills of any sort were undertaken, but after a few days route marches to Wimille and Wimereux were carried out almost daily which were very enjoyable. Rations were very sparse, however, and the cooks had more recourse to the tin-opener than the carving knife; and again the wily ones found that by being in the first sitting for meals they could get out by the exit and double round to the entrance and tail on the queue for the "second house". Credit must be given to the O.C. of the Camp in allowing the Troops to go into the town between 5 and 9pm and 3 and 9pm on Sundays, but a fly in the ointment was the fact that only ten francs were paid out per man, which did not admit of a very hectic life being led.

Most of this went on food, one delectable dainty purchased being French bread and lard. Gate-crashing in the cafes where music was provided was resorted to, but the proprietor, or as was mostly the case, the proprietress (Monsieur being away doing his bit) took a tumble. "You no beer? You buzz off!" – or words to that effect. Lady Angela Forbes' Canteen was a favourite resort of those who were not overawed by its fair Society helpers; but here again the wily ones found that with a little strategy dainties could be obtained and put on the slate, to be paid for later, and at the present time when there is great talk of War Debts perhaps there are some who have guilty consciences and believe in cancellation to ease them.

The Grand Column was a favourite spot to visit and on payment of half-a-franc a candle was handed by the 1870 Veteran in charge and up one climbed to see the surrounding country and the white cliffs of old England.

If the bulk of the men in the Camp had a soft time, one can look back and sympathise with those who were busy in the Orderly Room getting ready all the details to send us up again with the best of luck. No inkling could be got for some time as to our future, but our hopes received a little set-back when we were served out with "tin-hats" and gas masks. After some time we had a sort of General Post and found ourselves under the charge of Sergeants Stace and Henderson. I had as tent-mates Harry Musgrove and "Hinny" Johnson (later Camp Orderly Corporal); in the case of the former I soon found out where Manchester was on the map, and in the latter what a "Canny Player" was (this referring to a popular brand of cigarette).

Two items of great importance took place about this time – the collapse of Russia and the determined entry of the USA into the War. These two events gave us a great field for discussion.

At last the long-talked-of day came and the 31st paraded to move off. "Where to?" That was a jealously guarded secret which only a few knew. Rations were issued and off we moved to the station. After the usual wait we clambered into a train – "hommes-chevaux" as usual, and an R.O.D. loco appearing on the scene, off we started. Finally reaching Maroeuil, dusk found us with the Cotton Mill as our billet. This building, as its name implied, was a factory with many broken machines; but a space cleared for Troops to sleep, and we lost no time in

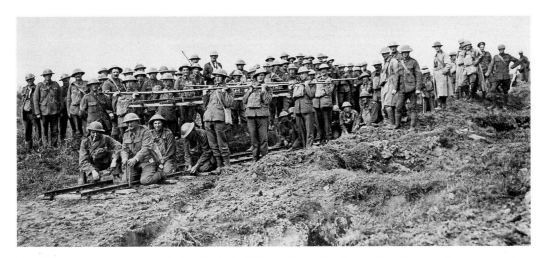

Tracklaying was a constant task for the Light Railway Operating Companies. For speed of construction, prefabricated track was preferred, this could be laid flat on the ground, with little preparation, and moved to another site quickly. Here, a new track panel is brought up by one party, while other soldiers bolt their panels in place. *(Museum of Army Transport)*

getting down to it. Morning came, and our first thoughts were naturally of our "innards". Unfortunately, during the whole time we were at Maroeuil something went wrong with the rationing and we had perforce to exist on voluntary contributions from other units to eke out the sparse rations from the Supply Depot. A pay-day eased the situation a little, but the money was soon swallowed up by the purchase of French bread from Mt St Eloi, a village a few miles away.

A mystery seemed to surround our future activities, but after we had been at Maroeuil a few days a Labour Company of "The Queen's" Royal West Surreys arrived and caused a diversion. They had rations in plenty and helped us a little with their "baksheesh". Several members of the 31st who had "Queen's" badges in their caps found their way into the meal queues until the Orderly Sergeant of the Labour Company discovered them a few days later. He was a sport, however, and did not send them away empty. "Come up an' arsk, and don't come the old tin man" was his remark.

After a fortnight or so, some of the 19th came to Maroeuil. The Canadians laid down some track and operating started with mules and a few wagons – but I will leave the description of this to a later page. Volunteers were sought for tractor driving by a 2nd Corporal, whose name I forget – he disappeared to somewhere from Maroeuil – and being rather tired of kicking my heels, I gave him my name. On parading the following morning, I was detailed by Sergeant Henderson to assist in the construction of a cook-house on the site of a new camp

Where more 'permanent' light railways could be constructed, conventional rail spiked onto wooden sleepers, and laid on a prepared trackbed, provided greater stability. Members of a Light Railway Operating Company – most likely the 31st – lay track at Feuchy in May 1917. *(Imperial War Museum Q5248)*

Hot soup is being brought up for the men in the trenches; a well laid 2ft gauge light railway is visible (right).
(collection – Keith Taylorson)

by the side of the railway, between a spur and the main line. A corrugated iron hut had been erected and our job was to fix up brick stoves for cooking. The first day was spent in collecting old bricks from around the vicinity. The same evening after a stroll, on the way home to the Cotton Mill, we walked along the track from Mt St Eloi to Maroeuil and on reaching the spur previously mentioned, by the side of the site of the new camp a huge shape loomed up in the darkness, which turned out to be a 12-inch naval gun on rail mountings. "There's going to be some 'doings' in this district" – and our prediction proved correct, as the following events will show.

Questioning the sentry as to whether the gun was in position ready for firing or only parked there, his answer was of a very non-committal nature. Next morning after the usual parade, presided over by the Orderly Sergeant, Corporal Ross (he of the lusty lungs), the bricklayers proceeded to the job. The 12-inch gun was seen to be manned by its crew, who were busy cleaning it. "Going to fire?" I asked one of the crew. "No, we are only resting here."

"If a Jerry plane spots that lot," I remarked to my companion, "we are in for a lively time." We settled down and soon were busily engaged in the construction of the brick ovens, a job I found very interesting. During the morning the "Archies" (anti-aircraft guns) were in action and bursts were seen in the sky above us. A Jerry plane was spotted. "That's done it! Jerry's seen this outfit. Hope we are not putting this up for him to knock down! Still, there's a War on and the Troops want a cook-house." So we applied our labours again.

A short time after there was a blinding flash, the ground shook as with an earthquake, and the cook-house collapsed on top of us. Extricating ourselves from the mass of corrugated iron we pulled ourselves together and found out the cause. The naval gun had started its share in the Battle of Arras, of which we were yet ignorant. Further work was suspended for the time, but on being informed that the Camp was shortly removing to the site by the gun, we had to start again with longer nails and past experience to work with.

Our usual routine was to proceed to the scene of our labours and ask the gun crew if they were going to fire. If so, we proceeded to the Y.M.C.A. Hut at Etrun for a spot of tea. If not, we carried on with the job, but watched them very closely. Ultimately, the Company moved to the site, but owing to its close proximity to the gun we afterwards moved to a sheltered cleft by the side of the Maroeuil-St Eloi road. Rations were still rather short and at this time a little incident occurred the mention of which will bring back a smile to all my old comrades who took part. The Labour Company of "The Queen's" was still occupying the Cotton Mill. A few days before the Battle of Arras commenced, our Artillery set up a very intensive bombardment in preparation, in which our old friend the 12-inch took part, sounding our Reveille in the absence of a bugler. A warning was issued by the Town Major to all Troops in Maroeuil, that in the event of the enemy retaliating heavily on the town, Troops were to proceed to Bray and take shelter in the village and huts there. The Officers of "The Queen's" evidently misread the instructions or got a bad attack of "wind-up," and instructions were given for all NCOs and men to go to Bray as the enemy were going to shell Maroeuil. It was an "every man for himself" affair and no arrangements were made to move stores, which were entirely abandoned. The sight of the stacks of rations apparently awaiting claimants was too much for the 31st and "scrounging" parties were soon on the scene joined by a few of "The Queen's" who had not been warned in the haste. The Camp that night presented a very festive appearance. Fires were lighted and the smell of sizzling bacon filled the air, whilst the ritual of "drumming up" was much in evidence. What the NCOs of "The Queen's" said when they plucked up enough courage to return can be imagined, but as knowledge is best bought with experience, Napoleon would no doubt have told them never to leave supplies in the event of a withdrawal. Any pangs of remorse we may have suffered were overcome by the taste of the excellent bacon and tea - real good Sergeant-Major's Brand.

Whilst on the subject of "The Queen's" Labour Company, I must recall one of their chaps who, being a little deficient mentally, was detailed as cook-house fatigue man. The main item of his job was the carrying of water from a well some distance away and on the journey back, to carry it up a 16-rung ladder. One day I noticed him return with two dixies (camp kettles) full, and was handed two empty ones to fill up. The moment he was out of sight the cook threw the water away. "What's the idea?" I said. "That poor devil has to carry that up a ladder." The cook became indignant and while telling me to mind my own business said "If we tell that chap we have enough water and haven't another job for him, he will wander off and we won't see any more of him for the rest of the day." They were a pitiable lot and we all regretted that it had been necessary to call them up and suffer the hardships of "over

A typical light railway train leaving for the forward area. It carries a mixed cargo of revettments, duckboards, sandbags and corrugated iron. The 'E' class wagons are packed to capacity and leave little room for the working party of troops from a labour battalion, who have to cling on wherever they can find a handhold.

(Imperial War Museum Q1699)

there". They were C3 men and were called on to do as much work in a day as they normally did in a week.

About this time rolling stock arrived and our first locos and tractors appeared on the scene. Where there are locos there must be coal, and an R.O.D. train arrived with several wagons of this necessity. The next morning we paraded as usual and the first allocations were made to the locos and tractors, these having been unloaded. The remainder of the men were marched off to the coal wagons. These were unloaded with shovels and a few curses, and at the end of the day the issue of a few banjos and clapper bones would have started a minstrel troupe right away. In the evening the Camp was divided into the Whites and the Blacks – those who didn't unload the coal and those who did – and I leave the remarks of the two factions to the memory (or imagination) of the reader.

The locos and tractors started operations – and our sympathies went out to the pioneers of the railroad in the last century. Track maintenance was in its infancy. We were all inexperienced in our jobs. "Off the road and on again" was the order and to run a mile and keep the track was an achievement. When somebody took a 20hp and a wagon to Artillery Corner and back without coming off it was the talk of the Camp, and was on a par with Bleriot's first flight across the Channel. Our method of working was the same as a single line tramway with loops. At first when two met in a section it was those who could argue the most forcibly who won the day, and the loser had to set back to the nearest loop or siding to allow the other to pass. Ultimately, up trains were given preference. Some very exciting incidents took place after dark. Coming off the road and re-railing was bad enough, but to meet a 20hp and some empty wagons head-on was a rather trying experience. To make two trips on a four-mile journey each way on one spell of duty was another achievement. One journey at night was the general rule.

By this time the Battle of Arras was well under way. We had a fellow feeling for the chaps marching up to go over in the snow and sleet as, like most of our big offensives in the War, the elements certainly did not favour us. The Artillery kept up one long incessant roar and it was some satisfaction to us to know that we were helping by taking up the ammo to within reach of the Batteries and relieving the congested roads, the primary function of the Light Railways.

With the advance of the attacking Troops, our track was extended and I remember driving one of the first tractors up to Roclincourt Valley. Somebody had had an excellent brain wave. We all left Maroeuil in a convoy, the idea no doubt being, that if all trains were kept together, sufficient help would be at hand for re-railing, or to meet with any emergency which might occur. My train consisted of three wagons of duck boards loaded end on in the wagons – i.e. upright – and giving the wagons the appearance of mobile huts.

We had a slow and cautious run to St Catherine's with only one derailment. Beyond this point the line had not been worked and was not ballasted, being laid in the valley (in order to be screened from observation by Jerry's balloons, no doubt) and was over ground softened by the heavy falls of rain and snow. We proceeded dead slow and the tractors and wagons pitched and rolled like boats in a rough sea. This proved too much for the load of duck boards – the two rear wagons pitched on their sides and the wagon next the tractor remained leaning over at an angle of 45 degrees, being kept up by its coupling to the 20hp Simplex, which refused to have its equilibrium disturbed. Sergeant Downs spoke very forcibly to me for allowing the wagons to topple over. Remonstrance was useless, any attempt at explanation being met with threats of being "put on the peg". Under his instructions the wagons were unloaded and re-railed and the material taken up in instalments. We arrived back at Maroeuil about 11pm, the journey having taken 15 hours to accomplish.

Our next day's trip was up the Scarpe Valley line to a spur behind the railway embankment. This was a very impressive run, and our longest and most successful trip so far, spoilt only by our having to unload the ammunition at the Battery to which it was consigned, as the guns were in heavy action at the time with no men available for unloading. The ground teemed with guns of all calibers, all thundering away and Jerry enlivening the proceedings with a return fire. The War was much in evidence in the air also, the enemy craft trying to locate Batteries and movements, with our planes trying to drive them off. We got away without any casualties and on arriving back at Maroeuil found we were moving to Arras the next day.

Chapter Two

"Q" Dump

Our journey to Arras was nearly on a par with scenes depicted in films of the pre-war era – of the early pioneers in the Middle West. We were journeying to the unknown; there was the element of danger ahead, and if there were no Red Indians there were the Germans after our blood, and in this instance we did not possess covered wagons.

We arrived and pitched our tents amongst the shells and fuses at "Q" Dump. For our neighbours we had the West Indies Troops, who were the Labour Company working at the Dump – finely built specimens of humanity and very cheerful, speaking good English. They were very popular with the British Troops in general, as they hailed from Jamaica where the rum comes from (Vintage S.R.D.).

Supplies and ammunition generally reached the light railways by way of the French and Belgian national systems. Interchange points were set up outside of artillery range where labour battalion troops – here a West Indian detachment – transshipped the supplies onto the narrow gauge. *(Museum of Army Transport)*

The Canadians had been very busy at "Q" and the layout of the yard impressed us very much, and we looked forward to commencing operations. No time was lost before we started in earnest. Most of the work was at night and our line extended from "Q" Dump – Fenchy and "Q" Dump – Athies, with spur lines branching off. The line back to Fosseux was worked by the 19th Company. The controls system was put in operation, District Control being established at "Q" and controls being opened at Ivory Junction and A.1. (Scarpe Valley line). Two shifts were organised for the operating staffs, which worked well as far as the control staff were concerned, but owing to breakdowns, derailments and track blow-ups, did not work well for the train crews – but more of this anon. On account of the heavy demands of the Artillery and R.E.s for material, we had a very strenuous time, as the Battle of Arras was still proceeding.

Our first two casualties occurred at this time. Private McKillys, a very decent fellow (transferred from a Scottish Regiment), was caught by an overhead telephone cable which had become unshipped, and was pulled off a wagon and thrown between the trucks. He was run over and subsequently died in Hospital. Private Burchell (transferred from the Grenadier Guards) was hit by a piece of shrapnel at Dutchman's Dump and was wounded in the arm. He went to hospital and we heard no news of him again.

Two very exciting events took place in these early days in the form of the Grenade Dump near "Q" and "Q" Dump itself, both catching fire.

In the first instance, I had been working trains up the Scarpe Valley line all day and on returning light to "Q" for relief in the evening, was stopped by Taffy Richards at A.7. and informed that owing to the Dump by the side of the canal being alight it was impossible to get to "Q". It was not pleasing information, as I had had only working rations consisting of a hunk of bread and a tin of bully all day, this being all the food we could get, it was not

Artillerymen prepare to unload shells from a train of 'D' class wagons at a dump near Bapaume on 23 March 1918. The ability of these wagons to carry a considerable quantity of large calibre shells is readily apparent from this view. *(Imperial War Museum Q8610)*

possible to work back to "Q" during the day. I was informed that several trains and tractors had gone towards Arras, but Taffy Richards could give me no information as to how they had fared as he could not get in touch with "Q". I decided to investigate, although the pall of smoke in the sky and the sound of explosions were not very encouraging. Getting as far as Blangy Bridge, I found the trains and tractors mentioned. After a discussion, three of us decided to chance it and run the gauntlet – if the track was not blown up. We set back and wagons were shunted into a siding, and Willie Macfarlane, Jack Williams and myself set out. When about half-way between Blangy and Arras a terrific explosion was heard, and unexploded bombs and pieces of casings peppered around us, some falling hissing into the river. My courage failed me and I pulled up and reversed, being the last tractor. The others went on, but I returned to Blangy and informed them of our experience. After waiting some time and the others not returning, I decided to chance it again as my "innards" called for attention. Visions of hot food being so near urged me on and I opened full out when nearing the danger zone. I skimmed across the trestle bridge at A.1. and the impetus took me up the incline to "Q" Dump in top gear and I reached the camp in safety. This was my fastest run on a tractor and I blessed the splendid maintenance of the track, it being laid on the tow-path of the canal.

An ammunition train arrives at a forward area artillery position near Brielen on 3rd August 1917. As there is constant danger from German artillery fire, troops wear combat gear and the guns (centre background) are camouflaged. In between the 'D' class wagons is one 'F' class, equipped with removable stanchions round which rope is tied. This type of wagon would only carry the smaller calibre shells. *(Imperial War Museum Q5854)*

The fire at "Q" Dump was almost as exciting. The night duty men had just come off and were waiting for the Orderly Officer and the R.S.M. (Downs) to inspect the tents (how we blessed this operation!). We were sitting having a hand of Nap when in burst one of the occupants of the tent, and grabbing a parcel of "luxuries" he had received by the Post that morning and his tin hat, he shouted "The Dump's alight! The Dump's alight!" and rushed out. We took little notice and decided to play out the hand we were holding before investigating, when suddenly a "pop, pop" outside made us sit up and take notice. We hastened out and found the cordite and fuses blazing fiercely. As self-preservation is a natural instinct, we "beat" it pretty quickly to safety on the other side of the canal. Luckily, the fire was prevented from reaching the 8, 9, 12 and 15-inch shells, and we returned to the Camp. We learned that 11 of the West Indian Troops had been trapped in a cellar and suffocated and several others burnt to death while attempting to escape. Sergeant Henderson of the 31st (afterwards C.S.M.) had performed good work with another NCO of the 19th in preventing the flames from spreading by clearing the boxes out of the way.

After this occurrence the Camp was moved to the grounds of a nursery on the St Catherine (Arras-Lens) road, and on this spot sprang up one of the most comfortable and best-equipped camps in France thanks to the efforts of the Officers and the splendid team work of those responsible for the fitting up of the Camp. I think most of the credit must be given

WDLR trains did not penetrate as far as the front line trenches. For transport over the last few hundred yards, trench tramways (also 2ft gauge), laid with lighter rail and equipped with smaller (usually hand pushed) wagons were used to distribute the ammunition. These trench tramway trucks are pictured at a junction grandly named "Oxford Circus" outside Arras in April 1917.

(Imperial War Museum Q5093)

to Captain Burge and Lieutenant Cannon, as I believe they were mainly responsible in planning and supervising the work. We started with tents, but by the time Autumn had set in, warm and dry huts were erected (how some of the stoves came to be in them will be told later). The food was good and a Canteen was opened, presided over by genial Corporal P. Elam. One of the huts was fitted up with a warm shower bath at one end and at the other facilities were provided for washing – zinc benches for scrubbing clothes on and for ablution purposes, hot and cold water being laid on. Another hut was fitted up for drying clothes, with lines run across and hot-water pipes run round the sides. An attendant was placed in charge of the baths (his name I cannot recall), and he was what the Canadians would term a "tough guy". He had roamed the world and needed little inducement to spin a yarn of the scenes of his many adventures. His job also was to receive the wet linen (?) which had been washed, hand a numbered chit for same, and hang the shirts, pants, socks, etc. (I don't remember any pyjamas) with a duplicate chit affixed, to be called for when dry – all in orthodox Cloak Room fashion. Most of us appreciated these facilities very much. It was a relief to be without our unwelcome guests who had roamed about our underclothing so long, and what soap and water could not accomplish a tin of petrol did, the petrol being used on the tractor afterwards without any detrimental effects.

The drying hut was also used as a Concert Hall, being cleared of clothes and the Canteen piano (a popular provision of the 19th Company) taken in. My Old Battalion was once in billets at St Nicholas and I was successful in getting permission for the Regimental Band to come along to the Camp, but Jerry started "cutting up rough" up the Line and they were called up. The next day the Battalion was moved suddenly to the Cambrai Front, to my great disappointment.

Other innovations at the Camp were an R.P. and Bugler, but owing to the different hours of duty the latter was dispensed with; or I faintly remember he was returned to the Infantry with several others when a shortage of man power was felt in the Line. One of those so transferred was later taken prisoner by the Germans during an attack and was put in a working party near the line opposite Arras. He managed to escape across No Man's Land and turned up in the yard at "Q" Dump, tired and hungry. He was given a feed and some "gaspers" and advised to report to the Town Major. This he did and was sent home to England.

Our first few weeks at the Camp on the new site were made rather uncomfortable by the over-zealousness of certain senior NCOs who were more intent on the military side of the business than the Corps aspect. Tent inspections was made a very rigid ritual and I had an unpleasant experience of this. Returning one morning from "Blighty" leave (the first for two years) very tired and hungry, and having that dejected, fed-up feeling with which only those who experienced it could sympathise, I dumped my kit in my place in the tent – sleeping in a tent always put me in mind of a jam (yes, very much sometimes!) tart, the place one slept in being the slice. I then went off to the Orderly Room to report that I was eager again to take up my activities in the successful advancement of the Great War. This being done I returned to the Camp to eat and rest, and found the Orderly Corporal and Corporal Girvan

All armies in the conflict made use of captured material, which sometimes included locomotives left behind in sudden retreats, or abandoned in no-mans land after breaking down. WDLR troops are pictured near Arras in May 1917 using a captured German Deutz petrol locomotive to haul a train of four wheel flat wagons. *(Imperial War Museum Q5253)*

waiting for me with the sad news that all the occupants of the tent were on the "peg". Result – R.S.M. Downs convinced Captain Burge so well that we got three days Royal Warrant. This was the only time my Copy Book was blotted in the 31st. I felt a martyr, but now, to use Mr Bottomley's famous remark, "I have paid, but –."

Things took a decided turn for the better when, following a difference of opinion in the Sergeants' Mess, a change took place in connection with several of the senior NCOs, and the welfare and work of the Company began to be studied more seriously. R.S.M.s Stace and Lummis tackled their jobs with great zeal and earned great respect.

Apart from the early days, life in the Camp was made as comfortable as possible; no irksome restrictions were in evidence, and so long as chaps behaved themselves no restraint was placed upon the occupants. We were placed on our honour and it is good to be able to say very few abused the trust. So long as one was ready for duty when required, it was possible to visit the Corps Cinema and the various Concert Parties "The Jocks" (15th Div.), "The Bow Bells" (56th Div.), The Guards' Divisional Party, the 55th and 41st, and the 33rd and 54th Divs., which were with us in Arras at different times. One could visit pals in the vicinity, the usual procedure if any distance had to be covered being to jump a passing lorry. Stopping and asking for a lift was rather risky, as very often an Officer was on board who naturally asked rather awkward questions.

Many of us have memories of Christmas, 1917, which was spent at the Camp. Every effort was made by the Officers and NCOs to introduce the festive spirit as much as possible, but three chaps were sitting enjoying their Christmas dinner when they were informed that they were required for duty. An hour later found P.E. 2026 busily shunting wagons in "Z" Dump. Snow laid on the ground, still silence all around, with the exception of a very occasional gun report or the distant rumble of a limber wagon – the results of the efforts of the few who did not believe in the policy of "Peace and Goodwill" for a few hours at least on the one occasion in the year. The experience was an uncanny one. Incidentally, it was the only Christmas I was with the 31st, I was transferred to the new Forward Companies just previous to Christmas, 1918, but by accounts when we returned the latter had been very enjoyable.

No doubt many of the 31st will remember Madame who kept the Estaminet on the by-road at the back of the Camp and which was reached by a short cut through the hedge, known only to a selected few. They will be interested to learn she was still there in 1929, having survived the last year of the War safely.

Yes! The Camp in the orchard at Arras was as much like Home as it was possible to make it, and when I left the Company to go on a Course at Berguette Works, I had an uncanny feeling that I was leaving it for good.

Jerry saw to that on March 21st, 1918!

Chapter Three

Operating

When we first arrived at "Q" our complement of power units consisted of about six or eight 20hp Simplex's, two or three locos and P.E.'s 1901 (The Yellow Peril) and 1902. The P.E. tractors had not had much scope at Maroeuil on account of the state of the track and the re-railing of these, what were then monstrosities presented a problem. (I think the experience gained in the early days helped pave the way for the later difficulties.) We were now joined by the 19th Company and our motive power was greatly augmented by a number of locos and 20hp tractors, and later on by more of the Dick Kerr (1901-2) type – Nos. 1907, 1936, 1937 – and locos made their appearance. Later, 2001 arrived, followed by 2004, 2024, 2026, 2034 and 2036, these being fine engines to handle. Early in the year 1918, the 40hp's arrived – very powerful but very uncomfortable to drive. One bore the inscription "Ot-az-ell", and a fitting appellation, too. Being boxed in, the driver had the full heat of the engine to contend with, the field of view was very limited, and if one had a blown joint, a goodly portion of

The 31st's staple unit of motive power was the 20hp Motor Rail or Simplex 4-wheel petrol locomotive. Simple and rugged, able to operate over the lightest track, and relatively easy to re-rail after derailments, the Simplexes were deservedly popular, and a total of 950 were built. *(Jim Peden collection)*

A large part of the 31st's duties were carried out using the 4-wheel petrol electrics built by Dick Kerr (Preston) and British Westinghouse Ltd. These were popular with the crews, being powerful and reliable, and having good cab protection (note the small side window). 1908 is one of the Dick Kerr machines, 100 of which were delivered in 1917. *(Andrew Neale collection)*

No. 2036 is one of the Westinghouse batch, also of 100 machines delivered in 1917. Although mechanically similar to the Dick Kerr locos, there were detailed differences in design, for example the lack of louvres on the engine access doors, and the front (rather than side) lookout window. *(Lens of Sutton)*

carbon-dioxide was swallowed, which in several instances led to the collapse of the driver. The 20hp's were the express units and the P.E.'s the slow (very slow on hills) freighters.

The duties of the train crews were at first 12-hour shifts. This did not work out very well in practice as when the power was in the forward area it was found most convenient from a traffic point of view to work up the ration and ammo trains, when darkness fell, without a change of crews; and when the latter had been out all day from 8.00am they were hardly in a fit condition to work until some time between 11.00pm and 2.00am whilst the relief were waiting at "Q". Steps were taken to obviate this by bringing on early crews, but still in many cases crews were working long hours.

Ultimately, a fine system was introduced to obviate this and it worked very successfully. A timekeeper was installed in a hut in the Camp booking the crews on and off duty, as required by the demands of the traffic. The control in the yard 'phoned that a loco or tractor crew and guard were required: the men who had had the longest spell off duty were called and booked on, and they reported for duty. This obviated standing by the engine or tractor when it was not in demand for traffic, but had the disadvantage of crews not being able to keep to a regular engine. This could not be avoided, and one had to be very wary when taking over to avoid a pitfall in the way of a not reported defect.

I have referred to P.E. 1901. This was the Jonah of the Company, the unridable mule of circus fame. If it went out on a journey and returned without having left the rails it was the talk of the Camp. 2001 was the gem of the tractors – fast and powerful and a pleasure to drive. On one occasion when working between Fampoux and the Chemical Works after dark, Jerry (no doubt having heard the tractor with his aircraft detecting apparatus) put up his searchlights, and no doubt his anti-aircraft gunners stood by, the warning having been passed on all round.

I have already mentioned the re-railing of the P.E.s, and one no doubt remembers the necessary tackle carried for this purpose: one or two bottle jacks, a traversing jack, ramps, crowbars, etc. – very handy after a derailment, but not very pleasant to be mixed up with when the tractor toppled on its side.

Another problem was the supply of pins and couplings. This will recall to memory the fact of the first out being the best equipped – the last getting hold of 18-pounder ammo box pins and other improvised couplings.

From the early days at Arras, the vast system of control boxes at passing loops and junctions was built up. The bugbear of letting up on caution was narrowed down and one could move more freely after dark without a train coming in the opposite direction and meeting head on. Blowouts were mostly found by experience, and points half cocked were usually the inevitable result of Artillerymen with push bogies and others who had been trying to acquire a working knowledge of the mechanism of railway points first hand.

This brings to mind the breakdown gang. Most drivers on the occasions when their help was needed, viewed their arrival with mixed feelings. Criticism was freely given on the cause of the trouble, but it was a relief to see them turn up. On one occasion their services were needed in the R.E. Dump at Ivory Junction in the middle of the night. The guard at the

Dump were very intent on witnessing the re-railing operations and failed to observe that stoves were being loaded into the off-side of the breakdown van. That is how some of the huts in the Camp were provided with Stoves, Lumber, Canadian, Mark II, but I have often wondered if the derailment was really accidental.

The question of food for the train crews was rather a problem at first. To start off with, when in Camp the usual meals were taken, and meals were brought to the yard for those on duty there. If a train crew were away all day it was difficult to keep check and friction with the night cook was usually inevitable. A cookhouse was set up in the yard to supply the crews with food – most of us will remember Addey the Cook, from Bournemouth. This alleviated the difficulty a good bit, but finally, with the "follow-up" system of booking on, a check was kept in the timekeeper's hut of all meals taken, and a chap who came off duty after a long spell was provided with a regal repast: *Rissole à la Fray Bentos; Pudding à la Tranchees; Biscuit à confiture; Fromage grande morceau;* Tea – R.S.M. Brand – a large pint; *Pain du beurre;* and if he could manage it, a Maconochie thrown in.

The locos Cooke, Hunslet and Baldwins did the lion's share of the haulage, but naturally being more or less in the back area, their drivers did not have the hair-raising thrills experienced by the tractor men. Apart from one or two trains getting out of hand when coming down the bank past New Zealand Siding into "Q" Dump, I think life was very settled in comparison.

The first of the 'main line' steam locomotives built for the WDLR were the Hunslet "War Office" 4-6-0T, A classic 'colonial' design with few concessions to war conditions.the class was nevertheless popular with British WDLR troops. No. 302 is the second locomotive delivered, ex works in August 1916. *(Lens of Sutton)*

Of the steam locomotives used by the WDLR, the most numerous class was the Baldwin 4-6-0T, mass produced from 1916 onwards. No. 883, one of a batch made in January 1917, displays the successful features of the class – its ease of accessibility, large spectacle glass giving good forward visibility, and open-backed cab for bunker first running. *(Lens of Sutton)*

A Baldwin in action, hauling a trainload of troops in 'D' class wagons, at an unidentified location. No. 743 was one of 90 locomotives of this type outshopped by Baldwins in December 1916. *(Lens of Sutton)*

The first American light railway units arrived in Europe prior to the delivery of their own locomotives and rolling stock, and many of their personnel had to be trained using WDLR equipment. This train of construction materials at a rear area location is hauled by WDLR Baldwin No. 780 and has US and British troops present. *(Museum of Army Transport)*

Mention must be made of Baldwin loco "Uncle Sam" and its genial driver, 2nd Corporal Walters, I think it will be agreed that this was the crack driver and loco of the 31st. Our old friend hailed from Cheshire originally I believe, but he had spent much time on the Canadian Pacific and the knowledge gained there stood him in good stead in France. The mention of the other side of the Atlantic brings to mind Sapper Baker and our old friends the Yanks who worked the "C" line. The former joined us at Boulogne. He came over from America and managed to enlist in the R.G.A., but being an American citizen he could only join by stating he was a Canadian. He was posted to a coast defence battery in England. This did not suit him, as he wanted to be in the thick of it. He had his wish by being transferred to a Heavy Trench Mortar Battery, was sent to France and when he joined the 31st he said he had seen all he wanted to and wanted to get back to America. He went on leave to London but did not return. Someone heard from him and he had a good job with the American Forces in London. We did not hear any more from him, and if I remember rightly Leave was stopped for a time as he did not return.

Most of us will remember our experiences with the Yanks. I remember arriving at C11 (Neuville Vitasse) one wet and cold night. Pulling up beyond the control box in readiness for the signal to shunt the train into the sidings, I waited for the signal, but apart from seeing a hurricane lamp being waved about no green side-to-side was forthcoming. Getting down from the P.E. I met the owner of the white light, who said "I guess you're a dopey sort of guy! Didn't you see my highball?" Explanations followed, the highball being correct American practice, and I spent many a pleasant moment afterwards while waiting for a train to work back to "Q" from the Yank's area. One of the "ginks" there had the photographs of

Another WDLR Baldwin 4-6-0T manned by US light railway troops takes on water at a servicing point.
(Museum of Army Transport)

The later arrival of the US light railway units into the war enabled them to benefit from their Allies' working experience, and the bulk of their "line" work was carried out using 2-6-2T locomotives, a wheel arrangement giving greater stability when running bunker first. This photo shows Baldwin 2-6-2T, No. 5127 at Rattentout. 100 locomotives of a similar design but built by Alco were in service with the WDLR. *(US National Archives)*

about 40 girls in the USA with whom he used to correspond. He must have been the equivalent of one of our lonely soldiers. To hear their conversation on the 'phone was a real entertainment, and on one occasion the non-arrival of rations caused some real ripe American slang to be put over the wires, to the great amusement of one 31st train crew.

Before closing this chapter, mention must be made of the sub-control posts and their occupants. Ivory Junction, one of the busiest, at which one always received the green when working homeward with relief at the completion of a day shift, and very often the information that the P.E. was to proceed to S. Arras to work the ration train to Monchy at this point. S. Arras Control, which controlled the traffic from No. 8 R.E. Park (Achiecourt). S. Arras Junction, with its triangle to S. Arras, Ivory and C11 (Neuville Vitasse). B305 – a warm corner whilst the 12-inch naval gun was there. B306, with its natty standard signal worked from the dug-out and the green or red light seen from a great distance. B308, Dutchman's Dump and New Zealand Dump, very warm at times owing to the heavy shelling there. B403, the last control behind Monchy and the Happy Valley line – the scene of many thrilling experiences and easily the most dangerous tracks operated by the

A view of the Scarpe Valley line, which ran for four miles from the basin at Arras to the lock at Blangy. In the background a train of skips hauled by a 20hp Simplex has just passed over a newly ballasted section of the line and prepares to attack a steep rising gradient. In the foreground are two boats operated by the Inland Water Transport Section, R.E. *(Imperial War Museum Q5829)*

Company. The first train over these lines after dark was always a nervy experience for all drivers.

Coming to the Scarpe Valley line, the track being laid along the towpath of the canal, it was a pleasure to work upon it, especially during the summer, and this line as far as Athies was singularly free from shelling all through. On a quiet, fine day, driving along under the leafy bowers of the tall trees overhanging the bank, it was hard to realise that a War was on. The amusing feature of this line was that the bank being a direct means of communication with the Front and Arras, it was much used by Troops passing to and fro. As no other means of transport passed along this way, the Light Railway was used as a welcome lift on the journey. Parties would collect and wait at the control points and although against orders, very few drivers could resist the appeals to stop and pick up between the controls. Officers, especially of the Guards' Division, showed their appreciation in a material form, and many a five franc note was changed at the Canteen, having come from this source.

The first control from "Q" was A1, beside the lock. On one occasion a 20hp with three wagons of wounded came across the trestle bridge which spanned the lock at the same time as a party of Troops were crossing. As there was no side clearance, most of them turned and ran back, except one chap. He jumped, or fell into the water, but could swim and was eventually hauled out with a rope. A2 was the next control and for some time a 20 h.p. was sent there from "Q" daily to bank trains over the Blangy Pimple – a very soft job and one much sought after. A7, the next, was an important junction controlling the various gun spurs behind the railway bank, the lines to Canteen Dump and Tank Dump, and the many gun spurs on the left side of the Valley. Tank Dump Control, another warm corner, was the scene of much activity after dark. The line from A7 was worked on caution to Athies, Fampoux and the Chemical Works.

The 31st was relieved of a great amount of traffic when the Inland Water Transport Section, R.E., put into operation the motor launches and small barges on the canal. The other trunk line, the "B" line, was operated mostly by the locos and was not used so extensively, except the area serving Dainville Yard, "X", "R", "Z" and Horseshoe Dumps. "R" Dump was elaborately camouflaged from aircraft and was in a wood. Netting with imitation leaves had to be lifted from the track before entering the Dump. Train crews were more or less hustled when working here as the O.C. had the fear that the presence of the tractor and wagons would give the position away to any aircraft which might pass over. This was rather a pity, as there was an excellent Y.M.C.A. near by, a fact which may explain the many slight defects that developed in the motive power whilst in section between B8 and B9. They sold excellent tea and biscuits there and an improvised dixie, consisting of a fuse or cordite tin, full of the steaming beverage was always welcome at any hour. This will be a piece of secret history to many, but we did win the War, anyhow.

Beyond B8 the line ran in long stretches between controls to Fosseux, but up to March 1918, had not been used very extensively. The controls were B7, B6, B5, B4, B3, B2 and B1. Up to the period mentioned, working this line was a welcome relief after being in the forward area and the run to Fosseux from "Q" was looked upon as a main line trip. Until a certain

R.S.M. was installed there, one could be sure of a welcome mug of tea and a bite to eat, provided by genial "Cookie" Jack Wingrove.

Between B306 and B403 the Tilloy line branched off. This long section served many Heavy Batteries, but owing to the absence of landmarks and the lack of controls (the amount of traffic did not warrant these) finding a Battery after dark was always an adventure.

The stretch of line between Ivory and Dutchman's was the delight of all drivers with a flair for speed, as being straight for about two-and-a-half miles and laid on broad gauge rails and embankment, it offered slight chances for coming off the road.

Spartan conditions were the norm in the (usually) temporary locomotive servicing facilities used by the LROC's. This quickly constructed shed lacks glazing or heating, but does include a shallow inspection pit. A Baldwin 4-6-0T is receiving attention from a large crew of fitters. *(Museum of Army Transport)*

Although not directly concerned with operating, the repair shops were very necessary adjuncts to this purpose. These were, of course, at "Q". Their work was carried out very efficiently, although under rather difficult conditions. Most of the men employed had to work with improvised material and several were on a different type of job to that to which they were accustomed in civilian life; but the results were good and the Company was fortunate in having Lieutenant Cannon to supervise the motive power.

Mention of the Shops Personnel brings to mind George Craigan, the tinsmith. In his leisure moments he did quite a business in the making of souvenirs. Give him a shell case and he would turn out a small coal scuttle or a vase. I wonder how many of us still possess evidence of his work in this direction.

LROC Maintenance Company troops show off the lifting capacity of their gantry, capable of raising a 14 ton Baldwin 4-6-0T off the rails. In practice this would usually only be necessary when moving a narrow gauge locomotive on or off a standard gauge wagon, for transport to another part of the front.

(Museum of Army Transport)

The night operations in the control hut at "Q" were at first carried out with the aid of hurricane lamps as a means of illumination, but in keeping with the standard of efficiency maintained by those in charge, the hut was fitted up with acetylene gas, the generator being outside. Some amusement was caused when the staff came off duty the first few mornings with black rings round their eyes, but this difficulty was overcome by washing the gas before burning by passing it through a water chamber.

Every main line railway company has its well known trains – as the "Southern Belle", "Eastern Belle", "Royal Scott", "Cheltenham Flyer" etc. The 31st was no exception to the rule and pride of place was given to "The Ration Train". This train consisted of a four-wheeled bogie, fitted up with a glass windowed body, which was dubbed "The Travelling Greenhouse" (and it did resemble one), "The Crystal Palace" and "The Directors' Special". The latter name was given it as it was constructed to convey officers on survey and inspection visits, for which purpose it was frequently used. When not so employed it was used to convey rations to all the control posts in the "safe" area over which the Company operated. In addition to rations, the letters and parcels for the control men were delivered, and orders were taken for commodities from the Canteen and the goods delivered the next day.

The driving of this train, usually assigned to a 20hp Simplex tractor, was a job much sought after, as it was one of the few trips carried out by this class of engine to Fosseux.

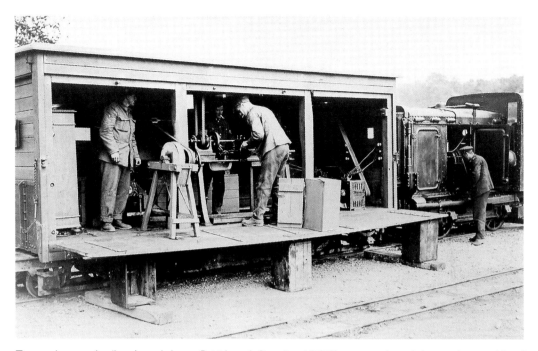

To supplement the 'base' workshops, British and Canadian LROC's operated workshop trains capable of carrying out virtually all types of maintenance to locomotives and wagons. This car is equipped with a lathe, other equipment included drilling machines, compressors and jib cranes. The complete train also included a generator car for providing power in the field. Motive power is provided by the Canadians' favourite type, a Westinghouse petrol electric. *(Canadian 'official' photo)*

An officers' inspection saloon, similar to the one described in the text, but belonging to a Canadian LROC, pauses while one of its occupants inspects progress on the digging of a gun emplacement in the Souchez Valley. A petrol electric forms the motive power. *(Canadian 'Official' photo)*

Two of the successful 'protected' Motor Rails, stored at a rear area workshop. One the left is No. 3022, one of the final batch, delivered in the middle of 1918 and consequently seeing little active service. *(Lens of Sutton)*

I am often reminded of the glass wagon by an old Infantry chum of mine whom I often see nowadays. He paid me a visit at "Q" Dump yard and spent a hour or so with me whilst I was on duty; when the ration train returned from its trip. I sent it to A1 to give him a lift home before it was shunted. Rather against orders, it is to be feared, but he was much impressed by the ride.

Chapter Four

Tales of the trains

The majority of the humorous events in life are closely allied to our misfortunes, and while at the time we are annoyed and hurt, to those blessed with a sense of humour the funny side becomes apparent later. Although a serious affair in most of its aspects, the War had its lighter side, and in this chapter I will recall several little incidents which, while serving to depict our everyday activities, will perhaps bring a smile to the reader – and to the persons concerned should they chance to read this.

On one occasion I took over a Westinghouse P.E., and ran the rule over it ready for a spell of duty. While engaged on this task Taffy Owen (acting as guard) came along and said we had to proceed to S. Arras with three bogie wagons and take a working party to their jobs on the Wancourt Line. Having arrived at S. Arras, Taffy went in search of the party and later came back with a party of Infantry consisting of a Lance-Corporal and about 30 men. On getting "line clear", we proceeded towards Wancourt as per our original instructions, *via*

A petrol electric locomotive hauls a trainload of men, probably on 'rest and recreation' leave, at a rear area location. Of interest is the timber viaduct, a relatively simple construction task for Royal Engineers, who trained in peacetime to build bridges like this from locally obtained materials. As with virtually all photographs of PE's in use, the locomotive is running cab first – much preferred by the crews, giving greater visibility, and earlier warning of track obstructions or defects. *(Imperial War Museum Q35476)*

S. Arras junction and Neuville Vitasse (C11). On arriving at the latter place I asked the Lance-Corporal where he actually wanted his party set down, and not being able to understand by his description, asked him to get into the cab of the P.E. and tell me when he came to it. I knew it could not be far along the line from C11, as the area round the curve was under enemy observation and work was only carried out at night in consequence. Off we started and on and on we went till the line took us amongst the numerous Batteries, which were blazing away and creating a terrific din. Every time I asked the Lance-Corporal he said "No, farther on," and eventually we reached the end of the line in Wancourt Village. The Lance-Corporal looked puzzled, but in the end said he thought it was about there and got his party off the train.

We started back and whether the enemy had seen us or not I don't know, but he started shelling and we had to run the gauntlet. I breathed more freely when we reached C11. Getting "line clear", we started off to S. Arras junction, where we were stopped by the red flag hanging outside the control. The control man came out and informed us that we had taken up the wrong party. They were C3 men who should have gone to Dainville and the party we should have taken consisted of Canadians who were engaged in construction work on the Wancourt line. So back we had to go and on approaching Wancourt found the shelling still pretty heavy. Reaching the end of the line again we looked for the party, but no sign of them anywhere. We asked the odd Artillerymen whom we met if they had seen the objects of our journey but without success, and after searching for half-an-hour without finding them we thought it more prudent to get out of the way of the shells and return. We were making our way to the train when we saw a head poking from a dug-out door and recognised one of the unfortunates. We found them gone to earth in several places, and after much trouble rounded them up and started back, with a salvo of shell-bursts to speed us on our way. When we reached C11, I held a Court of Inquiry, but to this day I don't know who blundered. Some of our comrades were very tickled when the incident was recounted to them later, but no humour was apparent to me while at Wancourt.

On another occasion, while driving P.E. 2024, I was hitched on to three wagons of bombs to take to the Chemical Works in front of Fampoux after dark. This tractor was one of four new ones posted to the Company. A few days after being placed in service a driver filled the petrol tank (he had overfilled it, as a matter of fact, and the petrol had run down the sides of the engine chamber) and it being dark he had used a hand-lamp to see if more was required – with disastrous results. Woof! – up went a sheet of flame and he luckily slid down without being hurt. Extinguishers were hurriedly brought into use and the flames put out. The engine was in the shops for some time as a result, but when being placed in service again started off with a tremendous jerk when sufficient electric current had been generated. This was very awkward when coupling up.

The guard having received "right away", off we started. Now the latter was an old friend, 'Erb Walmsley, and it will be remembered that he was the victim of an unfortunate incident. While driving a Baldwin loco light with two American Light Railway Officers on the footplate, in his endeavours to impress the Yanks with the capabilities of the 31st men in

Light Railway Operating troops became adept at repairing tracks, and rectifying the results of artillery damage, in an amazingly short time. The official caption for this photograph records that the track, near a location called 'Kit and Kat', was repaired and operable three hours after the 'disturbances' that had cut the line. The wagons have been blown off the line (though not seriously damaged) by the shellfire, and will be repaired for further use. *(Australian 'official' photo)*

driving, had a little mishap on a curve which resulted in the engine landing in a field at the side of the track. So as a result 'Erb was placed on the rear of the trains. Drivers usually requested him to hand over his lamp when working in the forward area on account of possible complications resulting from his use thereof, as 'Erb disdained the fact that there was a War on in the vicinity and insisted on strict L.&N.W. procedure everywhere. So I had his lamp.

We reached Fampoux and, having shunted a wagon, went on to the Chemical Works. On these occasions one usually proceeded until a guide or unloading party was sighted, but this time we reached the end of the track without seeing anyone. We were now between the Support Line and the Front Trench; but this did not deter 'Erb. "Hi! Hi! Who wants some bombs?" he shouted. I tried to damp him down, but his response of "What's up, 'Erb! Got the wind up?" reminded me that he was hopeless. The Infantry and Machine Gunners took a hand in trying to induce him to be quiet, but it took the threats of an officer to make him sit down and ruminate. Our unloading party turned up at last and when the wagons had been emptied we went back to Fampoux.

Having had orders to pick up some empty wagons which were standing in a siding, we stopped and set back for this purpose. Backing on in the dark was generally a tricky affair when wagons were already coupled to the engine, and stopping I shouted "How's that?".

"Back a little." came the reply. I set the controller and opened up the throttle, trying to allow for the peculiarities of the tractor resulting from the fire. Suddenly it gave a leap in the desired direction. "How's that?" – but no response, only a muttering in a moaning sort of voice. "Good Lord" I exclaimed to the brakesman, "I wonder if that knocked him down and he's been run over." We both got down and went to the rear of the train, fearing the worst. We found no sign of him, but shouting loudly we at last heard him reply from the bottom of the embankment, which was about four feet deep. We eventually found him scrambling out of an unusually deep shell-hole which was full of mud and water. Apparently he had been bending over to couple up, expecting the wagon to come back a few inches, and the sudden jerk had sent him down the bank into the shell-hole. During the whole time he was with the Company I never heard him use strong language, but I think he was very near to it on this occasion. Anyhow, I remember he criticised my capabilities as a driver very strongly.

On one occasion during the period of August, 1918, when the Germans were being pushed back, I was working a P.E. (No. 1937) with four wagons of wounded men bound for Arras from Wancourt, and while rounding the triangle at C11 the P.E. was rather badly derailed through a defective joint. I cannot explain the impulse that prompted me, but I pulled out the coupling pin and moment afterwards the P.E. toppled on its side down the bank. The brakesman and myself became mixed up with jacks, crowbars and the other implements we carried aboard. We must have presented a funny sight crawling out of the door of the cab more frightened than hurt. I remember this incident very well, as it was 14 hours before the

Amongst the first locomotives built for the WDLR were the 'Hudson' 0-6-0WT, as these were simply repeats of the well proven Hudswell Clarke "G" class marketed by Robert Hudson Ltd. The first twelve examples were shipped to France in June and July 1916. WDLR 107 (HC 1216/16) was photographed off the rails on the Albert to Fricourt road crossing in September 1916, providing a relatively easy rerailing task for the accompanying railway troops. *(Imperial War Museum Q4343)*

A train carrying the "never ceasing stream of shells" parallels the Menin Road, on the way up to the front line, on 3rd October 1917. *(Australian 'official' photo)*

breakdown gang arrived as at this time they had been working day and night carrying out hasty repairs to the track in order that material could be worked forward into the re-occupied territory.

Most of us will remember the Sunday when the Canteen Corporal obtained a very strong brew of beer from the Expeditionary Force Canteen. This had come from Switzerland, I believe, but it was responsible for a very hectic evening being experienced by most of the Company. We were working the 12-hour shifts at the time, it being about August, 1917. My shift went on at 8pm, relieving the day men. It was pay-day and the Canteen had been well patronised. I cannot confess to being a Canteen-wallah as regards beer drinking in those days, and then, as now, I only took a friendly glass. On this occasion, however, I had been induced to partake of a couple or so, which produced a mild kick – just giving me a slight merry feeling that enabled me to see the funny side of the events which happened later. We went down to the yard from the Camp and took over. The day shift joined the Camp and Workshops staff in the Bacchanalian feast.

Luckily, things were quiet up the Line and also it being Sunday (which was usually a little quieter than other days as regards traffic), apart from the usual ration trains very little work was to be done. The tractor drivers' and guards' hut, shunters' lobby and cook-house were all sub-divisions of a corrugated iron building, and this was where we spent the intervals between working hours. On this occasion it assumed the aspect of a meeting of a Rotary Club, and sparing the reader a lengthy description, these were my most vivid impressions.

Discussions, heated and otherwise, were taking place as to the best or oldest Regiments in the Army; the best railway in England; leave experiences; and between two individuals, one a Londoner and the other a Scotsman, as to who had served in the Army the longest. One beat the other by about 20 minutes, I fancy.

Two Scottish shunters sang native ballads as their loudest. An Irishman shook his fist in the direction in which we believed England to be, saying "If thim divils in the Houses of Parlimint was to be up there the War would be after being finished."

Jock Davidson went to sleep on a refuse box and an empty Machonochie tin was placed in his head and a broomstick in his hand – a caricature of Britannia.

A party of Guards officers came along and asked if there were any trains going along the Scarpe. They had been to the officers' club in Arras and they, too, were merry. On being informed that nothing was being worked that way, they asked if a special could be chartered. They offered 20 francs and, ever ready to oblige – this being the 31st motto, a driver was sent

Although many buildings in Arras were damaged or destroyed by shell fire, the town was not abandoned by the civilian population, and many restaurants, 'estaminets' (bars) and other diversions remained available to the troops in between spells of front line duty. This is the scene in February 1918, when General Newburn, the Canadian Minister of Militia, paid a visit to the town.   *(Canadian 'official' photo).*

off to start up a 20hp tractor. In the meantime, someone had produced a mouth-organ and being a Scotsman had started a reel. This suited the mood of the moment and many others joined in, the Guards' subalterns and the Scotsmen being in the fore. The dispatch of the train with its passengers ended the dance; then someone suddenly remembered they had a meal due to them. This led to a search for the cook by me, with the aid of a hand-lamp, as he was not in the huts. Eventually I found him sprawled across the broad gauge track (luckily for him, no Nord train came up that night). As he was not in a fit condition to cook I dragged him back and stepped into the breach and prepared some supper (Machonochies, bread and tea). After partaking of this, most of the shift settled down to sleep and the night passed without further incident.

We heard that the whole Camp had been merry, causing one of the officers to speak sternly on the matter, and the Canteen Corporal received instructions not to procure any more beer of the same specific gravity. It was a diversion, however, while it lasted and it was pleasing to know that nobody was placed "on the peg" as a consequence. This may have been due to the "Nelson at Copenhagen" spirit on the part of those in authority. If so, this spirit was

The British Army light railways actually penetrated into the streets of Arras and one line is seen here crossing a paved road and diving through a gap between two ruined buildings. A working party of Royal Engineers – in combat gear – is being conveyed in one 'C' and one 'D' class wagon, hauled by a petrol-electric. The date is 8th March 1918. *(Imperial War Museum Q8578)*

A French propaganda postcard, issued to illustrate damage done by German attacks, and showing the Rue St-Gery. A temporary light railway, installed to help with removal of rubble, can be glimpsed (centre).

(collection–Keith Taylorson)

appreciated. When work was intense it was tackled in a hearty manner by all concerned, and perhaps a little latitude was permissible at a quiet time.

It was to the credit of the Company that although pay-days were regular, only one or two overstepped the mark and received punishment. There was plenty of vin blanc and champagne to be had in the Town, and I well remember one large place in the street leading from the main square to the station. In pre-War days this place was (and is now) a rather sumptuous restaurant, but as the demand for lavish table d'hote dinners on the part of the civil population of Arras ceased during war time, it had been opened for the sale of vin blanc, biere and, other liquid refreshments to the British Troops. These were sold by the bottle only and the establishment was staffed by four women and two men, the latter, judging by their appearance, having been exempted from War service. The place was always crowded and there was generally some impromptu music and singing. It was quite an entertainment watching the crowd gathered there. At closing time one of the attendants rang a large hand-bell and all the staff started chanting "Finish beer! Policeman! Huit heure! Eight o'clock! Allez! Allez!" A couple of Military Policemen usually had to induce the stragglers to leave.

One evening, in the Corporals' hut in the Camp, Corporal Girvan mentioned the fact that it was his Birthday on the morrow. Somebody put forth the brilliant suggestion that the occasion should be celebrated and that a visit to the Canteen for drinks all round would be a very suitable means to this end. Being a teetotaller, Eddie Girvan said he did not favour the idea, but would book seats for "The Jocks" (15th Divisional) Concert Party at the theatre at Arras for those who would like to go. He went next morning and obtained the necessary tickets and arranged for the party to meet at the Corporals' hut at 6.30pm and all go together. Two of us were delayed on duty and were late at the meeting place. The remaining seven set off for the theatre, but five of them went in for some refreshment and lost Eddie Girvan in consequence. The two of us who were late off duty arrived at the theatre eventually, but as we could not see anything of the party we paid for admission and went inside, where Corporal Girvan and another chap had nine seats all to themselves. It transpired that the other five tried to get in by explaining that their admission had already been paid for, but a couple of Military Policemen having entered into the proceedings, their advice to "Get off!" was taken, and the five returned to the cafe and sought solace in France's national beverage (no – not coffee!).

Almost everyone who served on the trains can recall some narrow escapes. I probably owe my life to one chap who, through holding a different view, caused me to get off a 20hp tractor which a moment afterwards was badly hit by a shell. Reporting for duty at 8 o'clock one morning. I found my engine the only one available for service, the others being cut off by breaks in the track on both the Athies and Feuchy lines. I was detailed to bring back the breakdown gang from D305. The latter had been experiencing a very strenuous time during the night and the enemy shell-fire had been very severe in the neighbourhood of our track. A 12-inch naval gun had been firing from D305 and the Germans had not liked it a bit, and had expressed their disapproval in a very marked manner.

We arrived at our destination and found a P.E. with three wagons of ammunition, the former being in a large shell-hole in the track. The first wagon had been derailed, but by the time we arrived it had been put on again. The next job to be tackled was, of course, the P.E., but as a shell hitting the ammunition would have caused a worse disaster, I suggested to the Guard that we moved it away. He said it was not necessary and we started a mild discussion on the matter. I decided to consult the breakdown gang, who were taking a brief respite in the control dug-out, and the Guard followed. We had just reached the steps of the dug-out when a salvo of shells came over, the concussion of which blew us down the steps and we landed in a heap at the bottom. Other shells followed, but they burst farther away, and during a lull, feeling a bit hungry, I went up for some food which was in the locker of the tractor. I found the seat badly smashed and the bonnet riddled with shrapnel, but luckily the radiator, engine and gearbox were practically untouched and in working order. I could not help imagining what my fate would have been had I been sitting on the tractor. The German gunners apparently took a rest after this, as we had no further trouble. After we had drawn the wagons away, the P.E. was re-railed and the track repaired. We made our way back to "Q" and the battled-scarred Simplex created quite a sensation when we arrived.

Passing the spot where this incident happened was a breathless affair afterwards, but as the naval gun was pulled out a short while later we were not troubled again until the German Push commenced.

Chapter Five

The German offensive, March, 1918

During the first weeks of 1918 rumours were circulated concerning a great effort on the part of the Germans to break through the British Line, and any doubts as to the veracity of these rumours were dispelled by preparations being made behind our Front Lines for the demolition of bridges and railway tracks in the event of the effort being successful. Owing to the need for avoiding confusion and panic, secrecy was observed as far as was possible.

The enemy artillery fire increased in violence each day, being concentrated on such vital points as dumps, railheads, etc. Until this period, the immediate vicinity of the 31st Company's Camp in the orchard had been singularly free from shell-fire, but now the octroi and the yard were shelled by a large calibre gun, probably a 5.9, but luckily little damage was done. One shell fell into the Officers' Mess in the Camp but failed to explode and although bursts occurred all around, I believe this was the only shell which actually fell in the Camp. Another fell in one of the houses near the octroi and killed several men who were taking cover in the cellar, amongst them being 2nd Corporal Ogilvie, the Post Orderly of the 31st

The German Army had been using 60cm gauge Feldbahnen (light railways) since the start of the conflict. These would have worked round the clock in the period leading up to the German offensive in March 1918, when a massive build up of ammunition was needed. This view shows typical "Feldbahn" equipment, a Brigadewagen capable of carrying 5 tons, and an Orenstein and Koppel steam loco (right).

(Tony Steenmeyer/Utrecht/NL collection)

The German Army also used internal combustion locomotives in the 'front line' area. This is a useful view of a Deutz "Lokotraktor," used in large numbers by the Germans. The funnel on top of the bonnet is not the exhaust, but the opening of the cooling system for the 4-cylinder horizontal engine. The small wheelbase enables the loco to round very sharp curves. *(Tony Steenmeyer/Utrecht/NL collection)*

Company. (I have also heard he was killed in a cafe near the Oil Factory whilst in there for the purpose of having some refreshment, and I think this was correct.)

On the 21st of March the storm broke in its full fury and events moved quickly. The enemy kept up an intense rain of shells on Arras in order to hinder the movement of reinforcements and supplies. Then followed a very active and anxious week for all the personnel of the Company. An effort was made to maintain the utility of the line up to the last moment, and this resolve must have contributed to the final check. The idea of mounting field guns on light railway wagons, which had been tried out some time previously, proved to be of great use at this period, as they were taken into action at one spot, and after firing several rounds were hauled away to another point, this continuing *ad infinitum*. As the attacking armies advanced by reason of the rather rapid retirement of the Fifth Army on the Somme, it became necessary for the Troops in front of Arras to fall back in order to avoid the flanks being exposed. The Company still endeavoured to carry on. Troop and ambulance trains became the main items of traffic as owing to the movement of Batteries the delivery of ammunition was uncertain.

In a retreat, ammunition would often have to be recovered from dumps and moved back to a place
of safety. These Canadian troops are loading small arms ammunition into 'E' class wagons.
The dropside door, balanced on a couple of cases of ammunition, makes the job of loading easier.

(Canadian 'official' photo)

During the battles for Arras the light railways played a key role in moving casualties back to
dressing stations, where they received emergency attention, before being transferred to hospitals.
In the early days no specialised rolling stock was provided, so 'D' class wagons were quickly adapted
to carry four men on stretchers. This view is taken at Feuchy on 29 May 1917. *(Imperial War Museum Q5282)*

Contact between control points became out of the question as the retirement progressed, as the wires were continually being broken by shells and shrapnel and other causes. One epic message reached the control from B405 saying the Front Line Infantry were in the trench outside his dug-out – "What was he to do?" In the absence of official instructions the NCO in district control gave some very unofficial "advice". The R.E. Signals who were responsible for the maintenance of the telephone lines made superhuman efforts to keep touch with all controls. Often wrong lines were joined up in the confusion, and in efforts to ring up a certain control, "Q" would get in touch with Batteries, etc., who frequently replied in a very impolite manner. When contact was effected it was usually just in time for the control to ring up and ask for instructions, as the Infantry were retiring, and a few days after the attack commenced Ivory Junction became the last control in the forward area. But this did not mean that operating ceased beyond this point. Volunteers were not lacking to work up as far as was possible and while it is difficult to pick out special cases, it must be mentioned that Charlie Hughes (tractor driver) and Sappers Ridley and Walmsley (guards) did some splendid work at Dutchman's Dump handling Troop and Ambulance trains while under heavy shell-fire, and in two instances recognition was shown by the award of Military Medals.

The Canadian Construction Company and our own breakdown gang experienced a very strenuous time with blow-ups and derailments, and they both rendered wonderful service.

Another useful sphere of the Company's activities at this period was the transference of the stock to prevent its falling into the enemy's hands. As the area on the right of the territory operated by the 31st was the district most affected by the German advance, all the available stock was transferred to the 31st, and as the enemy came nearer to Arras much of the stock so received was handed over to the Company on the left, the 30th – for hauling to safety in the First Army Area, in which the defenders had been able to more or less stand their ground. When the Company moved forward to Bapaume and Cambrai later, much evidence was found to show how the light rolling stock had been worked back as far as possible and then rendered useless.

Locos and tractors had been run with throttles full open into dead ends, which damaged them almost beyond repair. The higher officials profited by this experience and later made trunk lines to the rear and fitted up the metre gauge system (which was in existence before the War) with a third rail to enable the stock to be worked back in the event of a further retirement becoming necessary.

One very smart piece of work was carried out near Arras. During the retirement, a loco had been left stranded and was at the moment between the opposing Front Lines. The breakdown gang went up and hauled it back under cover of darkness, leaving a very imposing dummy in its place, which at a distance looked the same as the one salved. Exactly why this was done I cannot say. There probably was a reason, or it may have been just one of those little spots of humour which were introduced during the grim days then being experienced. If the enemy had counted on panic being spread behind the British Lines, he was sadly mistaken.

To move wounded from the front lines, some four wheel wagons were adapted to carry two stretchers. Although the transport operation may have been painful, the speed at which the men could be moved to dressing stations by railway could often make the difference between life and death. *(Canadian 'official' photo)*

As the first few days passed, operating was also greatly hampered by the road transport endeavouring to make use of the light railway track. The roads themselves were badly congested and those drivers who tried the track as a quicker expedient found the proposition a more difficult one than they had anticipated, and blocked the track for its legitimate use.

As the flood of the enemy's advance made deeper inroads into the British Front and came nearer Arras, orders were given to evacuate the town. The civilians had been leaving for some days and shopkeepers who could not get their goods away in some cases gave them away, and others just locked up and went. Orders were given forbidding looting, but in the case of a shell bursting in a shop or cafe, it could hardly be called a crime to take foodstuffs and liquids. Men who had – and have now – great moral rectitude, had very few qualms when it came to scrounging (the verb "to scrounge" meaning to lightly take possession of). Whilst they would readily return any excess of change given them by a French shopkeeper, they would not hesitate to "knock off" any article which was apparently without an owner, or which was stamped with the hallmark of public ownership – W^D.

One such gentleman, who hailed from the land of the Shamrock, had an alarming experience in this direction. Going into an abandoned cafe, he became busy filling a sandbag with bottles of champagne, meanwhile keeping his eye upon the door for the possible appearance of the representatives of the smart Corps whose integrity could not be doubted – the Military Police. Micky was just on the point of leaving when to his great horror a Canadian Officer appeared from the cellar. "What are you doing?" he asked. Micky replied, "I'm after getting some of the bhoys a drink, as we can't get any because we are busy, and the drink-shops are indeed closed." As he said this he was wishing the ground would open and swallow him. A shell landing near would have created a welcome diversion. The officer looked him full in the face for a few moments. "Come here" he said, leading the way to the cellar. "When that chap comes to," indicating a Canadian NCO lying on the floor hopelessly drunk, "tell him the Battalion has moved to…" Mick returned later and tried to rouse the Canadian to sensibility but without success, and on returning again the next day found he had gone.

With the order to evacuate, the officers commanding the 31st and the controls were besieged with enquiries for assistance to move stores and equipment back. This was done as far as was possible, one of the biggest items being the huge stock of the British Expeditionary Force Canteen near "Q" Dump. So grateful was the Manager that he gave several cases of

By 1918 rather more sophisticated accommodation for wounded was being employed. This Canadian 'Red Cross' train arriving at the dressing station at Maroc is composed of 'E' class wagons and provides some weather protection for the occupants. Motive power is MR2128, an 'open' version of the 40hp Simplex. This has curved end sheets of heavy gauge steel, but no side protection and only an awning for a roof.

(Canadian 'official' photo)

stores to the Company, the contents of which were mainly disposed of at a very cheap rate in the Canteen, and for many days afterwards the personnel of the Company were walking about smoking cigarettes usually assigned to "Brass Hats", the humble Woodbine and like brands being then difficult to obtain. Rumour had it that the 15th and the Guards' Divisions lessened the stock of the EFC before going up to help stem the tide; but anyway, the Manager was very thankful to have salved what he did.

About a week after the commencement of the battle the decision to move the 31st was made. The Camp was dismantled together with the yard buildings and the repair shops equipment. This material was loaded and moved back to Fosseux, and the 31st was one of the last units, if not the last, to evacuate Arras. The loading was enlivened by the falling of heavy shells, and the passage of trains up the hills to B12 was made hazardous by the presence of one of our heavy Batteries by the side of the track. The officer in charge positively refused to hold fire while trains passed. Probably any injury which might have been caused by the concussion of his guns was of no consequence to him. One wonders if at any time he had cause to thank the light railway for his supplies of ammunition.

Arras was left with a pang of regret, as we had had many happy experiences there. With the move, away went most of our creature comforts, but throughout those very trying days credit must be given to the efficiency of the Quartermaster in keeping up supplies. Food was never short, although often it meant the contents of a tin instead of our usual supplies of fresh meat and bread, etc.

Eventually the last of the material was loaded and the remaining members of the Company climbed aboard and the train moved off. "Good-bye, Arras! What will be your fate?" It was being menaced again as it had been in the fateful days of 1914, when German advance parties had actually entered the town but had been driven out again. But the town was not to see the invaders again, except as prisoners, and these helped to clear up the debris after the Armistice. The Line immediately in front of Arras only gave way a short distance and the town acted as a bulwark against which the Germans spent their fury.

And thus the 31st left Arras; very few saw it again, as it was taken over by the First Army following the re-organisation caused by the withdrawal of the Fifth Army.

On our arrival at Fosseux, preparations were made for carrying on, which is described in the next chapter; but before closing, Sergeant Rattray recalls an amusing experience which occurred at this period. A wagon of timber was lost in transit and as the 31st had its good record of thoroughness to maintain, Sergeant Rattray went out to trace it. He eventually found the empty wagon standing in the yard at the exchange point with the American Light Railway Troops. The Doughboys were quite bland when questioned, but that did not deter George, and he found an officer and stated his enquiry.

Waal, I guess I can show you the timber alright." said the officer, and pointing to a smart-looking hut marked "Officers only." he continued "There it is, right there!".

Sergeant Rattray returned to the Camp deep in thought.

Chapter Six

The Turn of the Tide

From April to June, 1917, I was engaged in tractor driving, and from then until the institution of the system whereby crews were brought on duty as needed by traffic requirements (which was in November), I served as N.C.O. i/c. Drivers. After taking to the road again until February, 1918, I was transferred to the tractor repair shops, and after being there a few days was instructed to proceed to Berguette Works for a course of P.E. repairing.

After the course, on my journey back to Arras I was detailed to conduct a party of men to the Forward Transportation Depot at Savy-Berlette, near Aubigny. Here I was "collared" as an Instructor in tractor driving – much against my will, because I was anxious to return to the 31st. The Depot at Savy was conducted on strict Base Camp lines and did not appeal to me. I missed the friendship of my pals in the 31st, as well as the comforts of the Camp, and in spite of tempting offers of promotion I went to Arras one Sunday and asked to be claimed back.

It was during the time I was at this Depot that the break-through of March 21st occurred, and therefore I am unable to record the experiences of the 31st Company at that time. Of my own experiences I could write a lot, but as they hardly have a bearing on the subject upon which I am engaged, they are omitted. Corporal Steve Jennings had been sent to the Depot from the 31st as an Instructor in operating. Later, being attached for duty to the 1st Australian Light Railway Company, we got on the right side of the O.C. of the Company with such good effect that he arranged for us to return to the 31st.

While mentioning the Australian Company, it will be of some humorous interest to recall our first experience of their methods of working in comparison with those of the 31st. Reporting to the Company for duty, after the usual formalities at the Orderly Room we were sent to the cookhouse for refreshments. The R.S.M. was seated there with a mug of tea (special brew, of course) chatting with the cooks. The sound of a tractor drawing up outside was heard and a Sapper entered. "Say, Fred," he remarked, in the crisp nasal tone affected by the Aussies. "Sam's cutting up hell on that loco that's off the road, and says if you don't send someone up to relieve him he's going to pack up and leave it and come back." "Oh, alright." was the reply, "tell Harry Fraser to go up and take over, and I will get Bimbo to put it on when he comes back with his men." Steve Jennings and I could hardly control ourselves.

However, the Aussies were a good lot to work with, in spite of their seemingly casual methods. Yet we were eager to get back to the 31st. When we did eventually return, in the early part of May, the Company was at Fosseux, with the exception of the Tractor Section, which was at Bernville (B7), and to this place I was sent for duty. Lieutenant Grant and R.S.M. Gibbons were in charge. I was detailed for the job of night repairs – rather arduous

Baldwin 4-6-0T No 854 hauls a trainload of corrugated iron and track panels in a rear area location during the winter of 1917/18. *(Lens of Sutton)*

work by the light of a hurricane lamp, which had to be extinguished frequently owing to the activities of Jerry's night bombing squadrons, who were very busy dropping their eggs all round the district.

After a couple of weeks there, I was sent to the Third Army Repair Train, where my work consisted mainly of testing tractors after repairs had been carried out. After a fortnight or so of this, back again to B7. My chief work this time was driving Lieutenant Grant about with a small box wagon. I was chipped rather a lot by being called the driver of the Royal Special, but this job led to some amusing adventures which will be recalled later.

The Camp at B7 was in the middle of a cornfield, with a potato field adjoining. Corporal Woods (Micky) would take out his rifle and pot at the hares in the cornfield, and when the marksmanship of the Irish Guards stood him in good stead we had hare, new potatoes and pork and beans as a welcome adjunct to our rations. We had feeds of potatoes at all times and one day the owner of the field found out where his murphies were going. He attempted to blackmail us to the extent of 200 francs without success, and afterwards we resorted to the subterfuge of pulling up the plants, taking off the spuds and putting the plants back again. If they withered and died – well, that was the work of the moles, which were very prevalent in the district. Rather a low trick, one may think, but I was once asked half-a-franc for a mess-tin of water at Pont Remy during the Battle of the Somme.

Another memory of B7 was the earwigs. They swarmed everywhere. They got into the sugar in spite of the efforts of the cook to keep them out, and consequently they went into the tea when when it was made. They swarmed on the ceiling and when the cook lifted the lids of the dixies the steam caused them to drop off into the food. They swarmed over us in bed, but we never experienced a case where they entered a chap's ear and drove him mad, as the legend has it.

The bombing at night was very disconcerting. Matters were not improved by the tarring of the huts at the direction of the R.S.M., as this caused them to glisten very much on a bright night. It was not to his credit that he slept in a dug-out by the roadside half-a-mile away, leaving us to look out for ourselves in an emergency. On one occasion, a huge Jerry plane was brought down in flames, just missing the Camp, and in the rush to see it several of our chaps narrowly escaped injury from the exploding of the unexpended bombs, which were detonated by the heat. When daylight came an Air Force tender arrived to investigate. They examined the wreckage, but would not take away the bodies of the pilot and observer, as by their papers they gained the information that they had been engaged in the terrible raid on Abbeville. In this raid the W.A.A.C. Camps and Hospitals had been bombed very heavily, causing many casualties. As the reader will probably know, the Air Forces of both combatants buried with full honours all airmen brought down and who died in consequence.

On account of the disorganised conditions resulting from the German advance, no real routine work was being carried out at this period, and the traffic hauled was of a rather spasmodic nature. One morning I was instructed to stand by with a 20hp and a box wagon. Lieutenant Grant came along and said "To 'Q' Dump." A control had been established there in the cellars of the oil refinery, and to this place we proceeded. On the journey back I was told to stop at New Zealand siding, where an R.A.F. Officer and an Orderly were waiting. Together with Lieutenant Grant, they went into a nearby house and brought out a good many articles of furniture, which they loaded into the wagon. I expected the Military Police to appear at any minute, and had visions of being shot at dawn, or some milder expedient, for looting. However, they did not appear and under instructions I drove to Dainville, where the furniture was taken to the Kite Balloon Section's Mess.

On another occasion I reported as formerly and was told again " 'Q' Dump." On arrival there, Lieutenant Grant went to the dug-out to interview the occupants. The Germans started shelling the yard and I began to wish he would return so that we could start back. When he did appear he said "No. 8 R.E. Park." We drove there and when passing S. Arras Junction everybody was walking about wearing gas masks and shrapnel helmets. We had neither. I could not smell the gas on account of the fumes from the exhaust of the tractor. I wanted to stop and point out the fact to Lieutenant Grant, but was afraid he would think I was getting the wind up.

The 18-pounders, which had withdrawn to this position on account of the advance and were almost wheel to wheel, were blazing away and the din was terrible. I couldn't tell what was happening and had the wind up very much, but an occasional glance at Lieutenant Grant sitting there quite unconcerned, reassured me. We eventually arrived at No. 8 R.E. Park, which was practically deserted, being under enemy observation. We ran into the yard until a shell-hole stopped further progress.

Although the German railway troops endeavoured to move their locomotives and rolling stock back to safety during Allied advances, the speed of an advance, or the cutting of the line by shellfire, sometimes made this impossible. Allied shellfire has almost completely destroyed this 'Brigadelok' at Combles. Unusually the locomotive is an 0-6-0T: the bulk of the German roster comprised the ubiquitous "Feldbahn" 0-8-0T's.   (Imperial War Museum Q4763)

"Come with me, Heritage." – and I went, wondering what mission we were on. Lieutenant Grant seemed to be searching for something, and going to the other side of the Dump we came upon some chaps loading a lorry. Upon seeing our cap badges, their faces took on guilty expressions.

"What have you been taking, and have you an order?" They muttered that they had not, but had been given permission verbally to take the stuff. "Well," said Lieutenant Grant, "let's see what you've got." He ran the rule over the contents of the lorry and finally told them to take off some drums of tar and bundles of new sandbags, and directed them to carry them over to our box wagon. On the way over some Staff Officers hove in sight, coming in our direction.

"That's blinking (?) well done it." said Lieutenant Grant, pausing for a moment. "Still, we've got R.E. cap badges on." and off we went again. We saluted as we passed the officers, but luckily they did not stop and speak. The "fatigue party" loaded the tar and sandbags, the NCO was warned not to take anything without an order in future, and back we went to B7,

This German Army 60cm gauge train consisting of wagons loaded with logs has also been completely destroyed by British shell fire. *(Imperial War Museum Q4970)*

which we reached without further incident. By these means was the tar obtained – the tar which invoked the wrath of the occupants of the Camp at B7.

A few days after this incident I was told to take a tractor and driver to "Q" Dump, and that I would be in charge of all traffic operating in this area. Explicit instructions were given by Lieutenant Grant that in the event of the Germans advancing I was to go forward and collect all the wagons to "Q" Dump and when this was done to work them back farther still, if the rate of the advance allowed time, of course. However, we at "Q" had our own views of the utility of the tractor in such an emergency. The tractor was also to be used for banking purposes up the steep hill from "Q" to B11. Much useful work was done in this capacity assisting the trains which were working salvage and R.E. material from the dumps at Ivory, Blangy and No. 8 R.E. Park.

The Yanks had purchased (?) the huge fuel dump near "Q" and this was being worked back also. A Yank Sergeant was in charge of this and he was attached to us for rations.

Our billet was the cellar where the West African men lost their lives in the fire at the Dump. The top part of the building had been almost completely knocked down and we only had a concrete floor (or ceiling) about eight inches thick above us, which gave us qualms during the heavy shelling and bombing. A small shrapnel bomb from a plane burst outside the door one night, but luckily did not injure anyone. The cellar could have accommodated about 100 men and as there were only five of us we had plenty of room. Most of the cats which the civilians had left behind when they evacuated the town found their way into out billet – but we were spared the trouble of rats as a consequence. We gave most of them names "Dopey", "Rumjar", "Vin Blanc", "Cheesey", "Squibs" and other suitable appellations. The streets of the town were deserted, no movement of Troops being allowed in daylight, and bricks and fallen masonry were strewn all over the roads. I visited the well known resorts of our previous sojourn there. All the shops where we used to buy souvenirs and dainties were barred up or had been hit by shellfire. The Y.M.C.A. and Church Army and the E.F.C. were all locked up, and the Officers' Club in the Park near "Q" had had a big shell burst in it. The Park itself was overgrown with weeds, and bricks and a lamp-post had been blown into it.

When I visited this spot ten years later, I sat there with my wife and little daughter and thought how I had seen it last. The railings and seats had been repaired and repainted, beds of pretty flowers were all around, and a tennis court had been laid out. A couple who were of school age when the War was on were sitting, probably telling each other the age-old

Following a successful advance Allied troops often inherited sections of abandoned German railways. These were hurriedly repaired and connected up to the WDLR tracks, to help with with the movement of supplies forward into the newly captured areas. Canadian LROC troops repair damaged tracks at a location east of Arras in September 1918. A one wagon train propelled by a 20hp Motor Rail waits impatiently for the new rails to be connected. *(Canadian 'official' photo)*

story, and with these we were the sole occupants of this pretty little arbour. I wondered if they had seen it as I had during the War.

To resume. Time hung rather heavily on our hands. Cards were our chief diversion and we played kitty nap and whist for hours on end. The guns around us, the bombing planes and the shelling did not give us much chance for sleep. The daily visit of Lieutenant Grant was an event, and I recall two amusing events in which the latter was involved. His daily practice was to take off the receiver of the circuit phone and listen to the conversations which were involved in the working of the traffic over the area controlled by the 31st. One morning he overheard approximately this conversation. "Hullo, B10! This is Distant Control (B7) speaking. I am sending a tractor to pick up the four wagons in your loop...". "What! Bill Grant picked them up with his tractor and took them to 'Q'?" "What the ... does he mean by butting in and upsetting our arrangements," and probably some other fitting comments. Corporal Pearce recounted afterwards that on his return the officer in question strode into the control and said "Now look here, Pearce! Don't call me Bill any more over the phone. I won't have it!".

On another occasion he got off a train which then proceeded to the R.E. Dump at Ivory Junction. After waiting some time for its return he became impatient and walked along the line to meet the train. On the way a shell burst near him, blowing up the track. On his return to "Q" he informed us in his usual casual way what had occurred, and added "This blanky (?) War is no good for railroading, Heritage!".

About the middle of August things up the Line began to move in the right direction, and as at the time we were not aware that it was the beginning of the end, when orders were received to pack up and report to B7 we were set wondering what was in store for us. On arriving at B7 we found everybody packing up ready to move. Where to was a matter for conjecture as our destination was shrouded in the mystery of war. The next morning we loaded up all our tackle on bogie wagons. Trains were made up and off we moved – for all the world like a circus on tour. We were bound for at least a dozen places, but without any mishap reached Boisleux, the former headquarters of the 32nd Company (and afterwards of the Yanks), but this area had practically been abandoned on account of the breakthrough. There were a number of huts about, many of them damaged, but 2nd Corporal Carpenter and myself took possession of a small one which had evidently been used by an officer or senior N.C.O.

I well remember the first night there. Carpenter had gone on duty and I packed down to sleep. I was awakened by a loud crash. For a moment I wondered what had happened, but soon realised that a terrific thunderstorm was in progress. Now I must confess I don't like these things, having been unnerved by an experience some years before, and being alone did not improve matters. I lit a candle, when to my surprise I found the water coming through the roof. It had been well peppered by shrapnel and the rain was teeming through. Everything soon became soddened and there was no escaping it. I was cold and wet through and had difficulty in preventing the candle from being extinguished. How I longed for some of the rum I had spurned in days gone by! The storm lasted quite a long time, but at last dawn came. I crept out shivering, found a tin of petrol and some wood and started a fire in order to dry my most intimate articles of wear. On the face of it I should have contracted all manner of complaints; but no, I didn't even get a cold in the head.

At first our activities were very spasmodic as regards operating, but after a few days we moved again and camped in tents beside the line near Achiet-le-Grand. We again started operating in the Gommecourt area. District Control was now installed in a covered bogie wagon which could be connected up with the phone wires at the side of the line. Whilst working in this area, names of NCOs and men were asked for to take the place of the railwaymen who had gone on strike in South Wales. If my memory serves me rightly, almost all the Company volunteered, and we had visions of going back to Blighty, for a spell, at any rate. There was one Taffy in the Company who said he knew somebody who was acquainted with Lloyd George, he would get this somebody to speak to the great personage on the subject with a view to getting us all transferred to South Wales, indeed to goodness! However, a few days after giving in our names, the strike collapsed.

After only a short stay at this place, we moved again, and the Company was split up. The locos were stationed at Beaumetz and the tractors at Louverval. The former operated a large area in front of Bapaume and the latter covered the area towards Cambrai and Bourlon Wood, At this time, Cambrai was in German hands but was almost encircled by the British, and part of Bourlon Wood was still held by the enemy. It was at this stage that I finished my activities as tractor driver, although at the time I did not know it. I was detailed as Camp Orderly Corporal under a certain R.S.M. who was somewhat erratic. It was no sinecure when he was about.

Our first job on arrival was to pitch the tents and get a cook-house going. I was appointed deputy slave driver, but received my share of tongue lashing as well as the others. "Goanfetchthatmantherewhatsestandingthereforjumptoit!". Things had settled down a bit the next day, but operating had been in progress from the time of our arrival. Many had been on duty through the night and were sleeping the sleep of the just when the R.S.M. appeared and in his silvery baritone notes shouted "OrderlyCorpalallycorpallwanafatigueepartyeverymanincamp!" I went round and collected all the chaps waiting to go on duty – about six of them and reported to the R.S.M. He nearly exploded. "Isaideverymanincamp." "There's only the men resting." I replied. "Fetchemoutfetchemout." said he and I had perforce to drag them out half asleep. We went *en masse* to the yard (3 loops) and loaded the sections of a control hut on to a Bolster wagon, and were told to get aboard. Off we started in the falling dusk. After a long run a point near Bourlon Wood was reached.

The shelling was very heavy and guns of all calibers were flashing and banging, creating pandemonium everywhere. Limbers and wagons were going up in the air as they were caught by shells, and if we all had the wind up the R.S.M. had it worse. The driver stopped at a loop and informed us this was Bourlon Loop. After some time we located the control, with our old friend Atkinson working the phone in a shelter constructed of empty 18-pounder shell boxes. The R.S.M. took cover and we proceeded to unload the corrugated iron hut. When we had finished a bombing squadron of Jerry planes took a hand in the turmoil and bombs

Another train operated by a Canadian unit runs material up to the front line through a newly captured village. This well laid and ballasted line is of the more 'permanent' nature typical of the German 'Feldbahns.'

(Canadian 'official 'photo)

burst uncomfortably near. We wanted to get away so I took control and told the driver to start up. We were just getting under way when the R.S.M. came doubling up and tucked himself up on the bottom of the well of the wagon for the homeward journey, which was safely accomplished.

He had very little to say after this, but when he wanted a fatigue party I took care to warn all men who were resting that I would be coming round to collect a party and if they were about they would be wanted. Needless to say, they were missing when the time came.

Although things were pretty warm in the forward area, we had a quiet time at Louverval. Our Camp being by the side of the Bapaume-Cambrai road, we were able to gauge the activities in the line, and judging by the large numbers of German prisoners passing along to the rear we knew that things were going well for our Troops. Even then we did not realise the end was so near.

About the middle of October I was sent back to Bapaume, where Company Headquarters had been located, to take charge of the tractors which had been sent there (about nine in number and mostly of the 20hp Simplex type). On account of the large area being operated these were found to be the most useful with light loads on account of their speed. The chief work undertaken by the light railway at this period was that of moving up ammunition from the Dumps, which were now miles behind the Front Line, and taking it up to a convenient point. There it was loaded into motor lorries – rather a reversal of the procedure usually carried out before the advance.

A favourite run with drivers was that from Bapaume to Fosseux, where a small detachment had been left, carrying rations, etc. This run covered a distance of about 20 to 25 miles, and was always more or less an adventure as practically no controls existed in between. I remember making the trip myself, but driving a P.E. on this occasion. There had been rather a heavy fall of snow (I have since remembered that this was at the end of November, after the Armistice) and the trip made a lasting impression. We found the right track only with difficulty as nearly all the landmarks were obliterated and most of the journey there was accomplished in darkness. We had to charge into drifts in cuttings and the fouling bar on the front of the tractor pushed the snow away like spray from the bows of a steamer. Our chief difficulty was at level crossings, where the checkrails had held the snow, and the best expedient was to charge at them at full speed and trust to luck, or place sandbags under the driving wheels. The journey back next day was much easier as a thaw had set in.

One novel feature at Bapaume was the Blackstone gas engine which was used for pumping water from a well into an overhead tank for use by the locos. This engine had been installed by the British after the withdrawal of the Germans in the early part of 1917, was recaptured by the latter in their advance in March, 1918, and came into out possession once more in August of the same year.

I have strong recollections of this engine as, light repairs being part of my duty, I was often called out of bed in the middle of the night to get the thing started after it had failed. Wrong fuel was the main cause of these stoppages, but at this time we had to make do with what we could get. When these breakdowns occurred Taffy Griffiths, who was in charge of the pumping station, used to stand by and pour out a torrent of invectives in Welsh.

During the last few days of October, the arrival of the Continental *Daily Mail* was looked for each day on account of the good news which it reported. Bulgaria had signed an armistice, Germany was said to be seeking one, the Americans were throwing their weight against the enemy with success and we were advancing all along the Line. The news was very cheering, but we were afraid to be too optimistic. We fully expected another winter of activities and that possibly the Germans were retiring to another Hindenburg Line some distance back. In the Camp the opinion was that when a halt was made the Company would move up and carry on as before.

Then rather unexpectedly *the* news came. I had climbed into the top berth of the wire netting bunk which Eddie Girvan (the Camp Orderly Corporal) and myself shared in a dug-out in a trench, and was just about to fall sleep when in burst Eddie, shouting in his pleasant Glasgow accent "Heritage! Heritage! It's all over! It's all over! Wak up, mon, it's all over!". And he dashed out of the door again. Then the whistles of the locos started, one after the other, being tied back by the officers, until they were all in full blast, continuing until they eventually lost their head of steam some time afterwards.

I am reminded of this night of nights every New Year's Eve. Residing across the water opposite the docks at Woolwich, one never hears the ships' sirens and the docks locos.

without being carried back to the night of November 10th, 1918, just as the din and rattle of November 5th in London, with its attendant glare and firing of rockets, takes me back to the days in the Line with the Infantry.

I quickly got up and dressed, and made my way out into the damp, chilly air. Climbing out of the trench, I found that someone had started a bonfire, and a constant stream of NCOs and men were bringing up every conceivable thing that would burn and throwing it on the fire. Tins of petrol were included and excitement ran very high. Handshakes and thumps on the back were the order. "Now for good old Blighty! Peace at last! Peace! Peace!".

Looking back, I recall my mental sensations. The excitement calming down, the War as I had seen it passed before my eyes, and I drew away from the fire with a "Don't know whether to laugh or cry" feeling. My mind went to my old Infantry Battalion: what this meant to them, wondering where they were and what they were doing. A lump came into my throat when I recalled those who had "gone west". Fine fellows and good pals; and each Armistice Day – at the Cenotaph, the Bank of England, Southwark Cathedral, or any other spot at which I may chance to be – they come to my mind.

My reverie was suddenly shattered by a terrific crash which shook the ground. What had happened? Was it a "booby trap"? (These "booby traps" were explosive charges having delayed fuses, and were set by the Germans as they retreated; they were found in this area

One problem caused by the use of steam locomotives was the need for obtrusive water tanks, undesirable features as they made ideal 'aiming points' for enemy artillery. They could therefore be installed only in 'safe' rear areas. An unidentified Hunslet 4-6-0T poses alongside a simple, but professionally constructed, tower.

(Museum of Army Transport)

from time to time until well into 1919.) However, our doubts were soon set at rest by the news that a tunnelling company had set a mine in readiness for the event and had exploded it on receipt of the news, thus giving us all the last attack of wind up in the Great War.

The fire burnt merrily and the cooks got into action in the cook-house, the next day's rations being broken into for the celebrations. We had nothing stronger than tea available, but it warmed us up as the air was very chilly. One by one we eventually left the fire to go to our dug-outs and talk over the great news, afterwards seeking our beds for what little rest excitement allowed us.

The next day very little work was done. All thoughts were of our return to England. Almost everyone, if not all, thought it would be only a matter of a few weeks before we were demobilised, and Christmas at home was looked upon as a certainty. Had someone said that it would be nine months before some of us reached home, he would have been laughed to scorn.

Several weeks previous to the Armistice the tractor drivers were required to hand in their pay-books, and when they received them back they contained a new number and a mysterious entry – (in my own case) 231st Light Railway Forward Company. What this meant was a matter for conjecture. We had never seen or heard of the companies mentioned in the respective entries. What did it all mean?

We found out a few days after the Armistice. Myself and several others were told to pack up and a train was detailed to take us to Beaumetz. There we found the 231st Company, one of the old tramway companies which, under a new scheme, were to be half constructional and half operating for work in the forward area, the 31st and other like companies remaining behind to work with steam.

Several pleasant little stunts had been mapped put as part of our duties – gas trains, trench mortar and howitzer trains. We were to go up in a body, bump the enemy with the guns and mortars, send over the gas, and then return home to bed satisfied with a good night's work – if Jerry permitted. Speaking for myself, upon learning of these proposed stunts I was especially pleased that the Armistice had been signed.

And in this way I left the 31st – with great regret. I had spent my happiest days of the War with them. Being welded together from all regiments and with the 19th attached, we had worked as a team – all good pals and from the point of view of casualties, accidents and sickness we had been singularly fortunate. Our officers were of the best on the whole, treating us as we wished to be treated, with just the amount of discipline which correct military procedure demanded. The NCOs were the same when once the men had settled down to their work in earnest. If the few were over-zealous, and in isolated cases a little unfair, I am sure this is all forgotten and perhaps after-reflections on the part of those responsible have shown the error of their policies.

After I left, the 31st moved to Laboucherie and the 19th was split up and attached to various companies, the bulk of them operating at Marcoing. Being stationed at Velu with a detachment maintaining the R.O.D. broad gauge, I was able to visit them and I remember going on one of the joy rides organised on Sundays. On this particular occasion the 31st went

A petrol electric heads a train of 'F' and 'E' class wagons at a rear area marshalling yard. Troops on the adjoining lines are grading and repairing track. *(Museum of Army Transport)*

to La Folie to play the 19th at football. I took the opportunity to visit Cambrai instead of witnessing the match.

In February, 1919, the 231st moved to Vimy Ridge, and I saw the last of the 31st before leaving. We took over operating in a large area in this district from a Canadian Operating Company, who left for demobilisation. The area embraced Arras, Lens, Houchin, Bully Grenay, Vimy Ridge and the Labyrinth. Whilst working in this area, a strange coincidence occurred to me and a wish realised which showed the strange workings of fate.

In 1916 while with the Infantry, we took over the Souchez Sector on Vimy Ridge from the French, who were urgently required at Verdun. The area behind this Front was served by the Decauville track, by which name it was then known. When I first saw it I was greatly interested, and I remember saying to a comrade "That's just the job I would like." Little did I dream that this system would be extended and worked behind the whole Line, and that I would be engaged on this work and finish up my War service in this area.

It was with a thrill of pleasure that I recognised the very spot where I had first seen the narrow gauge in operation (at Verdrel) when on my first trip to Houchin to draw rations in the capacity of Acting Q.M.S. for the Half-Company which had moved from the Cambrai area. I could not resist the temptation to ask the tractor driver to allow me to take over on the journey back and drive the 40hp Simplex over the old familiar ground where my wish had been voiced, half in jest, three years before.

On the arrival of the second half of the 231st, Corporal Disley and myself had charge of the district control, and after a few months I left on demobilisation for England, home and beauty, with thoughts of old pals miles away with the 31st.

Introduction to Chapter Seven
by Capt. T. Barty

The 19th Light Railway Trains' Crew Section – to give it its official designation – was formed at Bordon in February, 1917, and left there for France on the 15th day of that month. After a lapse of almost 15 years many incidents are forgotten and only a few are impressed upon the memory – the night journey to Folkestone and the arrival there at break of day, expecting to be in France before noon, but told to go to billets and report next day. The three days hanging around Folkestone; the arrival in Boulogne, the uphill march to St Martin's Camp, the mud and slush there; the depression caused by the issue of "tin hats" and gas masks. The early start in case we should miss the train at Boulogne, the wait for hours before it started, the wonderful speed at which it ran; the arrival in the darkness at Avesnes-le-Comte, with no one expecting us. The march to Wanquentin and the finding of billets in a farm-yard. The erection of huts at Fosseux which we expected to occupy, but which were given to another Company – and so on.

Then the laying of the light railway on chalk, more chalk, and again more chalk as it subsided and the locos toppled over. The rushing of ammunition towards the Front for the battle of Arras. The arrival of the Life Guards at Wanquentin on Easter Sunday; our awakening at daybreak on Easter Monday by the drum fire which announced the commencement of the battle.

Each day brought its incidents – many humorous and mostly now forgotten; but one outstanding incident was the day when we suddenly saw great clouds of smoke rising from the Wanquentin ammunition dump and heard the tremendous explosion a few minutes later which told us that the dump had gone up; the disappearance of many heels over the horizon and the bombardment of exploding shells, small arms ammunition, etc; and the really interesting moment when we were turning in for the night after a welcome issue of rum and the usual Jeremiah remarked "There's 700 tons of gun-cotton in the dump to go up yet!"

Shortly afterwards the Company began to be broken up into detachments which were sent to work with other Companies. Those of us who remained were later sent to Pozieres to clear salvage from the 1916 Somme battlefield. In the course of this work we saw many places that were previously and afterwards immortalised as the scenes of great battles, and it seemed then that destruction could not be more complete. We little thought that the Boches would be there again in a few months' time.

Whilst at Pozieres I received orders to transfer to another branch of the R.E.s, and I said "Good-bye" to the 19th Company with great regret.

As I know that the conditions under which the Company worked after that date became much more strenuous than anything I had experienced, I have written these remarks with great diffidence.

An improvised locomotive shed apparently adapted from a group of farm buildings, with three Baldwin 4-6-0T's awaiting their next turn of duty.   *(Museum of Army Transport)*

I am glad, however, that I have this opportunity of paying a tribute to my brother officers – one of whom, alas, is gone – and to all other ranks in the Company. I am proud to have commanded, even for a short period, such a fine body of men, who did such excellent work; and who, by their cheerful acceptance of whatever conditions they had to undergo, well maintained the traditions of the British Army.

It has been a great pleasure to meet old friends at the Annual Re-unions, and we are much indebted to Mr Heritage for the hard work he has put in organising these. It is a wonderful tribute to his energy that over 50 members of the 19th and 31st Companies were brought together at the 1932 Re-union, and we hope that still more will be present in succeeding years.

Chapter Seven

The 19th Company

Difficulty has been experienced in obtaining sufficient details to write this part of the book, and through the painstaking methods of our friend W. Hill I have learned many interesting items concerning the 19th which are quite new to me. He has made a study of facts connected with railway operation during peace and war, and possesses a wealth of both mental and written information on this subject, items of which have been very useful in compiling this book, especially the Appendix.

I have sympathy with the members of the late 19th Company from the point of view of *esprit-de-corps*. Going to France as a Company, they were afterwards split up and attached to various other Companies, such as the 31st, and in the happenings mentioned in the preceding portion of this book the 19th played a part, helping to make the 31st Company what it became – a highly efficient body of men.

I should have like to have recorded some of the experiences of the officers, NCOs and men of the 19th who were attached to other Companies, but although several promised to write, only "Bill" Hill gave any information, and he was mostly with the 31st. So if this part of the book does not seem to give the credit which is due to the 19th, the facts mentioned must be borne in mind.

The 19th was formed at Bordon during the latter months of 1916 and was composed mainly of railwaymen recruited from the British railways. If they did not get the intensive military training that most of the 31st men had, tribute must be paid to the fact that they endeavoured to carry out efficient railway operation even under the most difficult circumstances – a factor which helped greatly to attain the desired object.

Of the actual formation of the Company and any details concerning the life in Camp at Bordon I have no information, so will pass on and let W. Hill give an account of the Company leaving England and their subsequent adventures.

□ □ □ □ □

"Fall in the draft!".

The stentorian voice of the Sergeant-Major resounded over the parade ground at Bordon.

It was late in the evening of one day early in February 1917, and small groups of men could be dimly observed falling into position. After being addressed by some "brass hat", who informed us that we were "badly wanted overseas to work the railways, and so help to bring this disastrous War to a speedy and successful termination," etc., etc., the 19th Light Railway Company marched off on the first stage of the great adventure. Truly, we were a cosmopolitan crowd – men from Devon and Cornwall, some from Lancashire and Yorkshire intermixed with Tynesiders, Scotsmen, Irishmen, Welshmen and men from our colonies; but nevertheless, all one big family.

We entrained at Bordon and after an all-night journey reached Folkestone. Whilst there we were billeted in boarding houses on the Marine Parade, and stayed three days, being unable to cross over to France on account of fog and the submarine menace. Eventually we got across and took the long trail to the ever popular (?) St Martin's Rest Camp on top of the hill overlooking Boulogne.

We left Boulogne next day by train, being loaded up in the celebrated 8 *chevaux, 40 hommes* wagons, eventually reaching Frevent late in the evening. We changed trains there and boarded a metre gauge train. After about an hour of this we detrained. This night was one of the few unpleasant memories we experienced – raining, falling over unseen obstacles, we floundered along like a flock of lost sheep. After eventually being sorted out, half the Company were detailed to rest in a stable and the others were more fortunate in getting into a Salvation Army Canteen. We found out next morning we were at a place called Avesnes-le-Comte.

After breakfast (?) we paraded and marched off, led by Captain Barty and Lieutenants Hire and Cannon and our old friend Sergeant Gibbons doing all the shouting. After tramping for about five hours we reached Wanquentin, eight kilometres away (it was suggested afterwards the Sergeant had the map upside down).

As a result of difficulties with water supply, many WDLR steam locomotives were fitted with water lifters, to enable water to be taken from rivers, streams and the ubiquitous shell-holes. Baldwin 4-6-0T No. 788, so fitted, double heads with a Simplex 40hp tractor on a train containing track panels. *(Lens of Sutton)*

We rested at Wanquentin for two days and then proceded towards our destination – Fosseux. Here the 4th Light Railway Company joined us, and we were provided with picks and shovels to help lay the railway from Fosseux to the outskirts of Arras. We thought of the parting words at Bordon – we had to make the railway before we could work it!

Whilst this work was in progress, some of us were sent as a detachment to Maroeuil to relieve the Canadian Railway Troops. When we arrived there we were well amongst it – eight o'clock at night, hungry, and no earthly idea where we were to be billeted. Anyway, someone found an old dilapidated estaminet and in that place we decided to make ourselves as comfortable as circumstances would permit. One or two tried to light a fire and the rest went on the scrounge, eventually returning with some spars of wood, wire netting, nails, an old hammer and a rusty saw. At about twelve o'clock we were on the way to getting some beds up. Unfortunately, only two of us apparently had any knowledge of carpentry (probably the onlookers had vague ideas of quartermasters' jobs). I think one of the carpenters threw the hammer at a chap who asked a silly question regarding the speeding up of the work. Railroading there was a curious business. The motive power consisted of mules – six to a truck, with an R.F.A. man in charge of each animal.

We were at Maroeuil about six weeks previous to, and during the second battle of Arras. Then the 31st Company came on the scene. Their arrival was, of course, the signal for the departure of the 19th, who packed up and marched back to Fosseux, via Avesnes-le-Comte, led by Lieutenant Cooke (afterwards killed).

We joined the 4th Company at Fosseux in March 1917. During the time the 19th had been away, the light railway had been laid to South Arras, spurs having also been laid to the dumps at "R", Horseshoe, B9 and "Z". All the controls from B1 to B13, "Q" Dump, were open, also posts were established at Blangy, and Ivory Junction. The men of the 19th Company were billeted in Nissen huts at Wanquentin until the time of the dump explosion there, an incident which caused our first casualty. Corporal Truman was hit by a piece of shell and died of the wounds.

Somewhere about June, 1917, we moved *en bloc* to Pozieres, on the Somme, being conveyed by motor transport. Captain Barty and Lieutenant Hire accompanied us. On arrival there we again took over some huts which had evidently been occupied by our predecessors, the 29th Company. Nothing had been left in the shape of material, but we eventually found a small Pechot loco, No. 202, in a somewhat dilapidated engine shed; but this did not dishearten us, as we soon set to work and made some rolling stock out of wheels, etc., which we salvaged from shell-holes. A few Hudson locos were sent us later, and we managed to carry on fairly well. We were salvaging at Pozieres, and the line ran to Aveluy, Courcellette, Ovielers and Moquet Farm in the one direction, and Contalmaison and Bapaume in the other. We were fairly comfortable there and stayed about two months.

Then came another move, this time by light railway to "Q" Dump, Arras, to join the 31st Company who were in charge there. On arriving, the 19th Company was once more split up and several of us went on to Fosseux again. Loco 532, two train crews, a cook etc., carried on there for a time. The original yard at Fosseux had been converted into an ammunition dump and our work lay in supplying this from the dumps at "Z", "R" and "X".

Our small party eventually rejoined the main body at "Q" Dump. By this time the 19th Company had ceased to exist as a distinct unit, the bulk of the men having gone to strengthen the 4th, 6th and 9th Companies, which were operating around the Bapaume and Fremicourt sectors. The 54th Company who were at Basseux operated the lines to Saulty L'Arbret, Ransart and Monchy-aux-Bois. We linked up with them by a branch line from B5 (Simencourt Junction) to Beaumetz Junction. We carried on at Arras until the 20th Company came. Then we moved to Wailly, taking over the sector which the 1st American Engineers had been working. This line ran from Beaumetz to Boisleux-au-Mont, Henin Junction, Boyelles, St Leger, and on to Ervillers.

I was stationed at Henin Junction control from September 5th to October 10th 1918; Boyelles, October 11th and 12th; Achiet-le-Grand, October 13th, Bapaume, October 14th and 15th; and the Armistice found me with the 3rd Army A.D.L.R. at Bancourt.

The 19th Company, I understand, had been reformed as an operating company at Rocquinoy and finished its career at Marcoing in October, 1918.

Thank you, Mr Hill! You might have told us more, but the printer is asking for his copy, so we must let it go at that. I might mention that Mr Hill wrote a very interesting article for the L.M.&S. Magazine on "Light Railway working during the War". It consisted of 48 pages of foolscap, but was not accepted on the grounds of its being too long. In this he gave a description of the early days at Maroeuil, when the light railway went through the same evolution as the railway in England during the early years of the last century. I have written up the following from the article in question:

After being at Fosseux about a fortnight, 23 men of the 19th Company were detailed to proceed to Maroeuil to relieve about 100 men of the Canadian Railway Troops who had been on construction and operating (?). We arrived at about eight o'clock pm, and after some difficulty found a shelter for the night. The next day we went to the yard to commence operating and received rather an unpleasant surprise. The only rolling stock we could find was in the shape of a few old French bogie wagons, and enquiries revealed the fact that the motive power was – mules (0-2-2-0).

When we started work, this was our daily procedure. Procure a wire cable with a loop on one end and a hook on the other. Find the wagon and mules, the latter with an R.F.A. driver to each pair, six mules being the usual number. A brakesman was provided for turning the wheel at the other end of the wagon. There were no formalities as regards getting "line clear", and persuasive argument ruled the road. When hitched on "Right away!" was given to the leading driver. Then the fun commenced. In dry weather, clouds of dust, and in wet weather, showers of mud and clods of earth, were thrown up by the mules' hoofs over the unfortunate brakesman. When going down hill or in stopping great skill was necessary to prevent running into the mules, as they had a nasty habit of kicking with their hind legs, and some dexterity was required to avoid these kicks. The worst the locos did in later days was to

Between 1914 and 1918 the majority of the British Army's supplies, ammunition and indeed artillery was horse-drawn. Vast quantities of fodder were needed to feed the animals. This train of 'E' class wagons drawn by a Hunslet 4-6-0T shows bales of hay stacked as high as they can go. Perhaps for safety, the accompanying troops prefer to ride on the less comfortable sheeted loads! *(Imperial War Museum Q35518)*

shower ashes and sooty water over the brakesman. Whilst being unpleasant, this was preferable to being kicked.

Where the line ran beside the road, as it did in this area, at night lorries and wagons encroached on the track and we became mixed up in traffic jams. In consequence, if the track was not damaged the points would be put out of action by mud and stones, and had to be cleared out with a stick before we could proceed.

We usually started at about eight o'clock in the morning and a journey to Mt St Eloi or Anzin generally took about six or eight hours. After a mid-day meal another wagon was taken, the journey being completed between 10.00pm and 2.00am Derailments were frequent and on one occasion our train caught up the one which had preceded us. Its guard was standing by very disconsolately as his motive power had vanished. The rope had become unhitched and a few shells having been pitched overboard, the drivers and mules had got the wind up and bolted. So the wagon was coupled to ours. After unloading at our destination (Madagascar Corner) the return journey commenced, and presently Jerry began shelling the road. The rear bogie of one of the wagons became derailed, but as the drivers either could not or would not stop it bumped along for two miles, finally being completely derailed at a set of points at Anzin Church. After about five weeks of this mode of operating, the first batch of 20hp Simplex tractors arrived and we gladly said farewell to the mules.

Mention of the mules becoming unhitched reminds me of a later incident. During the descent of an incline after dark, I noticed the speed of the train was much faster than usual, and was just clambering over into the wagon in front of the rear one on which I was riding, in order to put on the brakes, when a figure loomed up from the wagon, shouting "Put on your brakes, we've broken away!" We managed to stop the train and found the loco and one wagon missing. Suddenly there came a crash in the rear and we found a P.E. (2036) and one wagon of ammunition had run into us. However, nothing was derailed and the P.E. propelled our wagons to the next control point, where we found the loco waiting.

Our friend very aptly describes the Control system in the article mentioned, and as it has not been detailed in the section dealing with the 31st I will extract it in brief, putting in various essentials to make it more complete. Each Operating Company had its District Control (in the case of the 31st at "Q" Dump), acting on instructions from Central Control, which gave orders from a Corps officer who was concerned with the traffic to be moved. Instructions received from this officer were passed on by Central Control to the District Controls operating in the areas concerned.

All statistics relating to the tonnage and mileage, fuel consumption, repairs, rolling stock in use and available, track damage and accidents, etc., etc., had to be rendered by the District Controls to Central Control, and if Tractor Driver X had what he termed a "rough shunt"

WDLR units were adept at using available materials to build and improve the railway infrastructure. These Canadian troops are loading rubble from buildings ruined by artillery fire; this would then be lightly crushed and used as ballast to consolidate or extend the narrow gauge tracks. *(Canadian 'official' photo)*

by being required to perform a long spell of duty, while he blamed the District Control for what seemed to him their inefficient method of working, it was generally through a German shell being planted in the middle of the track perhaps some miles away, so bottling up power and rolling stock which would have otherwise performed the job he had to carry out.

Orders having been received by District Controls as to what troops and material had to be moved, they were passed on in turn to the Sub-controls spread out all over the system.

Trains leaving the District Control were under their supervision all the time. This control was fitted up with a bevelled rail which represented all running roads and a clip was provided for each loop and siding. An order for a train crew would be passed on (at first to the NCO i/c shunters in the yard, but in latter days to the timekeeper at the Camp) and the loco or tractor would back onto its train. The guard would take the names of the driver and brakesman (or fireman), time on duty, loco or tractor number and wagon numbers, and these, together with his own name, would be handed to the District Control. "Line clear" would be obtained to the next control and the train would start.

A clip bearing the above particulars would be moved along the bevelled rail to the next section; and so on as the train moved about as directed by phone from the District Control. Where wagons were detached or picked up these were put on or taken from the clips bearing the corresponding numbers or names of these points. French names of places were avoided as far as possible in order to confound the enemy intelligence agents, and on many light railway systems English names were given to the various points. In the case of the 32nd Company's system, names of stations on the G.W. Railway were adopted, such as Swindon, Taunton, Newquay, etc. As far as the 31st was concerned numbers and prefix letters were used, a system which was, in my opinion, the better.

Sub-controls had to inform District Control when wagons were loaded and unloaded and acted as representatives of the Company in their respective areas, and also had to give particulars of wagons in their sidings three times a day.

District Control staff worked in three shifts of eight hours each. Sub-controls were each manned by two men who usually made their own arrangements, but officially, I believe, were on 12-hour shifts. In the forward areas they were housed in small corrugated iron huts, and in the back areas dug-outs were requisitioned. In each case two bunks, a table, stove and portable telephone were provided. The men in the forward areas did most of their work by night, and while one man attended to the phone the other would be out controlling the traffic, which was very intensive after dark. As the forward areas were often under continuous shell-fire and also the site of gun emplacements, it is a mystery how the control men managed to get their rest amidst the roar and din. Much could be written of their adventures, but these few lines will bring back to the memory of the reader who was in the Service, or to the imagination of those who were not, the difficulties of railroading with the products of German and British munitions factories arriving and departing.

Speaking figuratively, the light railway delivered the ammunition to the door of the battery, in a larger bulk and in a shorter time than the motor transport, thus releasing

Much routine maintenance of WDLR locomotives had perforce to be carried out in the open. Here a Baldwin 4-6-0T (identified from its works number as WDLR1061) receives attention on a raised inspection platform at Westenhoek. *(Museum of Army Transport)*

the latter for the work of delivering ammunition to isolated batteries away from the light railway area.

Train crews were often chipped by the Infantry, reference being made to a cushy job. The light railway personnel did not suffer the hardship and danger which befell the Infantryman; they had food and shelter to which to return, and were able to keep themselves clean and free of vermin. All the same, the job was no sinecure, as jobs went in those days. A train of ammunition was not a comfortable place when shells were bursting near, and operating in the forward area was generally a nerve-racking experience; in the Monchy areas, the track ran to the support line of trenches, and at the Chemical Works beyond this line.

In concluding this chapter, I should like to mention that had I had more information upon which to work, I would have been pleased to have made it a more lengthy chronicle of the activities of the 19th Company. Probably when these lines appear in print much interesting material will be forthcoming. However, though this chapter be small in comparison with the portion relating to the 31st, it will, it is hoped, serve as a lasting souvenir of a fine Company; one which, if it never entirely had a wheel of its own, in a figurative sense, put its shoulders to other wheels and helped bring success to their united efforts.

Chapter Eight

Apres la Guerre

Settling down after the War was a strange experience, even to those who had jobs to which to return. One missed the old routine of ordered things, and for a while the experience was like one long leave from the other side; but gradually the threads which had been dropped were taken up again. The old spirit of comradeship was missing and it was found that being with workmates and colleagues for a few hours each day wasn't quite the same as being together for 24 hours, living and working together and experiencing the hazards of War. Meeting an old Army pal seems different, and it is this feeling which gives so much pleasure at Regimental Re-unions. In cases where a unit was recruited locally, the meeting of old comrades in the street occurs frequently; but with units like the 19th and 31st Companies, which were composed of officers, NCOs and men drawn from all parts of the British Isles (and in a few cases even farther afield), such meetings can rarely happen.

In my own case, somewhere about the end of 1919 I met Tom Foy ("The Demon Brakesman", to give him Corporal Disley's appellation) at Plumstead. He was carrying home a package of fish and chips, and as the family wanted it with some degree of warmth still in it, he could not stay long to talk. He informed me, however, that he was shortly going to New Zealand – he is probably there now. On another occasion I saw Mr Cannon at Brighton, but circumstances did not permit me to make myself known. I also met Sergeant Leach and 2nd Corporal Denman at Victoria. Yet another was Sergeant Rattray, whom I met on the District Railway in London, and as he frequently worked the train upon which I travelled to and from work, I was able to exchange incidents of the old days with him. Sergeant Wells I saw from the top of a bus upon which I was travelling on another occasion, but he was lost in the crowd before I could leave the bus. Putting down my money for a ticket at Moorgate Street Station one day, I was greeted with "Hello, Corporal! How are you going on?". The questioner turned out to be one of the famous pair who were at A5.

These were the only members whom I met, with the exception of Penton whom I met at Victoria Station. Whilst attending the Re-union dinner of the Infantry unit I served in previous to my being transferred to the 31st, I thought of old comrades of the latter Company and decided to try to organise something of a like nature in order to bring some of them together for an hour or so. Accordingly, I sent off a notice to the *News of the World* for insertion in their Comrades' Column. The next day I came home from work hoping that the postman had been busy. He had, as there were several letters awaiting me. Great was my disappointment when I found they were from caterers, entertainers and musicians, all eager to secure orders for the proposed Re-union. Similar letters continued to arrive for several days, but no response came from old members.

After a lapse of two years, I met Sergeant Rattray and we talked over the possibilities for a Re-union. He was as eager as I and it was decided that if only a few could meet it would be very enjoyable. By a strange coincidence Mr Cannon's address was sent along to the place at which I was employed, for registering purposes. So I wrote to him, and to my great pleasure he replied very enthusiastically on the subject, and asked me to pay him a visit. With the encouragement and assistance received from him I determined to go "all out", and as a result of published notices and a little detective work 27 of us met at the "Clachan", Kingly Street, Regent Street, London, in February, 1931, and spent a very enjoyable evening. The pleasure of those present was very apparent, and the Chairman (Mr Cannon) and the Vice-Chairman (Capt. Barty) both voiced the general opinion that the event be held annually.

In consequence, 57 sat down to dinner in February, 1932. Most of the officers were present, including Captain Burge, Captain Lovatt and Captain Murray, and Mr Webster looked in during the evening. The esteem in which the officers are held by the other ranks and *vice versa* was very apparent. Old memories were revived and forgotten names recalled. The spirit of comradeship was in the atmosphere and the meeting finished with "Auld Lang Syne".

To be present and witness the results of my work in helping to bring together those who were there was more than a reward for the labour involved. I feel I must record the generosity of Mr Cannon in covering the incidental expenses of these Re-unions, together with the help both given and offered by W. Hill, G. Rattray, and many others. I hope that in the absence of someone more fitting to take on the job, I shall be privileged to arrange many more Re-unions of the two Companies, and it may be possible to arrange a trip to Arras in the future.

And now, in conclusion, let us venture a peep into the future.

Year: 1960. Scene: A West-End restaurant. A young waiter escorts a party of very elderly, white-haired or bald-headed men to a table.

"Your table, sirs. What will you drink with your dinner?"

Orders having been taken, he retires to execute them. Another waiter asks him "Who are those old buffers at that table?" The first waiter replies "Some chaps who worked the railways in the War they had years ago" "Oh, that War! Fancy people going about killing each other.

Let us hope so!

Appendix One

The following details of the track and rolling stock (with the exception of those relating to the tractors) have been taken mainly from records compiled by Sapper W. Hill during the time the Companies were in operation, and have kindly been passed on to me for inclusion in this book. I, like many others, regret not having kept a diary, and although this practice was strictly against orders at the time, the Powers that were will no doubt now forgive Bill Hill for this breach of military discipline.

Track

Gauge, 60cm (1ft 11.5 ins). Weight, 16 to 20 lbs per yard. Bolted together with fish-plates and spiked direct to sleepers with dog hooks (as French standard gauge). Ballasted with chalk and sand mostly quarried in the area where laid.

Tractors

20hp Simplex; 40hp Simplex

Made by Rail and Tramcar Co., Bedford, England. Fitted with Dorman engines, chain transmission. Two speeds and reverse; former about 5mph, latter about 20 to 30mph.

Petrol Electric

Nos. 1901 and upwards, built by Dick Kerr, Stafford. Fitted with 40hp Dorman engine coupled to a dynamo transmitting electric current to motors on each of the two axles. Nine speeds and reverse, but not effective in use over third gear as current was not powerful enough. Weight, about 10 tons. Required very good track upon which to run.

Nos 2001 and upwards, built by British Westinghouse Co., Trafford Park, Manchester. Fitted with 40hp Dorman and 45hp Tylor engines. Otherwise specification as No. 1901. Controller more suitable than that of the latter, also much lower petrol consumption and kept track better. Weight about 9 tons.

The radiators of the P.E. tractors became very hot when running cab first as they relied for cooling upon a forced air draught from a fan. This fact was turned to good account by the train crews, who found the hot water thus provided very useful for making tea and warming tinned meat and vegetable rations.

After the Armistice when the demand for tractors for haulage purposes practically ceased, they were found very useful for lighting camps, the leads to the motors being cut out. The 20hp tractors were also very popular after the Armistice for joy-riding and touring the devastated areas. I could quote a case where an NCO was away for a week exploring with one of these engines. All this by the way.

Locomotives

Baldwin

Built by Baldwin, U.S.A., 1916-1917. Wheel arrangement, 4-6-0. Cylinders, 9ins. by 12ins. Coupled wheels, 1ft 11^1/$_2$ins. Coupled wheelbase, 5ft 6 ins. Steam pressure, 178lbs per sq in. Boiler diameter, 2ft 9ins; length, 7ft. 83 tubes, each 1.5ins diameter. Total heating surface, 254 sq ft. Water capacity, 396 gallons. Coal capacity, 13cwt. Weight in working, 14.7 tons.

Having no rear bogie, this class of engine had a tendancy to leave the track when working bunker first.

Cooke

A much better and more powerful loco than the Baldwin. Built by American Loco Co, USA, 1916 to 1917. Wheel arrangement, 2-6-2. Cylinders, 9ins by 14ins. Coupled wheels, 2ft 3ins. Steam pressure, 175lbs per sq in. Boiler diameter, 2ft 8ins; length, 8ft 3ins. 54 tubes, each 2ins in diameter. Heating surface, 272 sq ft. Water capacity, 396 gallons. Coal capacity, 15cwt. Coupled wheelbase, 5ft 6ins.

Hunslet

Built in England. Splendid-looking locos, conforming to British standards in appearance and build, and more solidly and soundly constructed than the American locos. The Gresham injectors fitted on these locos gave little trouble in comparison with those fitted on the Baldwin and Cooke types.

Wheel arrangement, 4-6-0. Cylinders, 9.5ins by 12ins. Steam pressure, 160lbs per sq in. Boiler diameter, 2ft 9ins; length, 5 ft (?). 86 tubes, each 1.5ins in diameter. Heating surface, 205 sq ft. Coupled wheels, 2ft. Bogie wheels, 1ft 6.5ins. Coal capacity, 15cwt. Water capacity, 375 gallons. Weight, about 14 tons. Coupled wheelbase, 5ft 6 ins.

Hudson

These locos were mainly used for shunting purposes and were rather skimpy in appearance.

Wheel arrangement, 0-6-0. Cylinders, 6.5ins by 12ins. Steam pressure, 150lbs per sq in. Boiler diameter, 2ft 1in; length, 5ft 6ins. 45 tubes, each 1-5/8 ins in diameter. Heating surface, 126 sq ft. Wheels, 1ft 11ins in diameter. Coupled wheelbase, 4ft 2ins. Coal capacity, 3cwt, carried in small bunkers at sides of cab. Water capacity, 110 gallons carried in a tank under the boiler, between the frames, thus differing from all the preceding locos., which were side tank engines. Weight of loco in working order, 6.5 tons.

These locos were very powerful for their size, but were not suitable for service away from their depots on account of their limited coal and water capacities. When in use, however, they were fitted with a small tank wagon as a tender with a hand pump fitted.

The Hunslet, Baldwin and Cooke engines were fitted with suction pipes for drawing water from streams and other suitable sources, but as overhead tanks were erected when the system was developed, they were not used very often. At first, however, it was frequently found necessary to draw water from shell-holes and ditches, but owing to the possibilities of choking, this was rather a risky procedure.

Barclay

This type of loco was built in Scotland and closely resembled the Hudson type, the specification being to all intents and purposes, the same.

Wagons

The standard wagon was of an open box type, the body being 17ft long, 6ft 6ins wide and 3ft 6ins deep, mounted on two four-wheeled bogies, the ends of the bogies projecting beyond the body about 1ft 6ins. There were coupling slots, and a brake wheel operating on two wheels. These wagons were the "D" class and were the most efficient for all-round work, having drop sides. The "C" class were French wagons, about 10 ft. long with two four-wheel bogies and a side handbrake, but were not very numerous.

The "E" class wagon was almost the same as the "D" class, but had a well in the centre. It was very difficult to re-rail these wagons when they had left the metals, and they were awkward to load. Many of them were converted to "D" class by boarding the well over. The "F" class were similar to the "E" but had open sides and stanchions for carrying timber and rails. This type was used for the mounting of guns, which could be fired without being dismantled.

The "H" class were like the "F" but without the well, and fitted with a tank of about 1,600 gallons capacity, in which water was conveyed for the troops in the trenches or for loco purposes.

The average weight of the bogie wagons was about 30 to 35cwt.

The "A" and "B" classes were four-wheeled box wagons about 6ft by 5ft and were used for carrying rations, and officers and patrols for inspection purposes. They were not as numerous or useful as the bogie type. During 1918 a good many covered wagons were handed over for service. These were built in England. Their class letter is not known, but they were similar to the "D" class, except that they had bodies about 6ft 6ins in height with middle and end sliding doors. There were also swinging brackets to take six stretchers each side, for use when on ambulance work. These wagons were also used as mobile controls, being then fitted with phones and desks and could be connected to the phone wires running at the sides of the track in a very short time. After the Armistice they were fitted up as living vans for light railway units, stoves being fitted in the centres.

What happened to the light railway equipment after the War would make very interesting reading if all the facts could be obtained. An effort has been made to get together some details from various sources but without very much success. It has, therefore, been necessary to fall back upon my own observations and to seek assistance from Mr Hill on the subject. No doubt many of the small items, such as watches, handlamps, etc., were bought from the Disposal Boards by the home and foreign railways. Most of the track was left down and together with some of the rolling stock was used by the French in reconstruction work in the devastated areas. I saw a 40hp and something like 30 wagons in use at "Q" Dump, Arras, in 1922, and the light railway was being used for transshipment from and to the Nord broad gauge. Most of the sidings, however, were taken up.

The 20 and 40hp Simplex tractors were bought up by various contractors at home and abroad, together with some of the steam locos., and were used in construction work on the many new arterial and by-pass roads which have sprung into existence since the War. Whilst cycling to Folkestone in 1922 (en route for France) I saw a properly organised system of light track being operated for many miles along the main road, which was being widened, and the track reminded me of the old days in the 31st. The tractors still bore the old L.R. number plates, but the wagons were of the four-wheeled tip-up type, similar to those used by the Canadians in construction work. These wagons were very handy, as I have memories of being able to re-rail them single-handed when empty, and two men could carry out the same operation when loaded. But for the fact that the drivers and engines were very much soilstained, I could well have imagined I had ridden into the War days again.

I saw many Simplex tractors in use on the Upminster extension of the District Railway, and also on a system which had been laid down to carry materials from the broad gauge in connection with the building of the vast housing estates of the London County Council at Becontree, Essex, and Downham, Kent.

Most of the P.E.s seemed to vanish without leaving any trace, but a number of them were standing in a field near Ashford, Kent, for about six years. They could not have been much good after having been exposed to the atmosphere for so long, but whether the engines and electrical equipment had been taken out I cannot say.

As regards the locos, they are still to be seen, and if anyone wishes to be reminded of the old days, it is possible to take a trip behind one in various parts of the country. The Ashover Light Railway and the Lynton and Barnstaple Railway (owned by the Southern Railway) are two instances. It seems strange that these engines which once carried officers and men to and from the strife and din of modern warfare, are now being used to carry, in many cases, the same beings in pursuit of their peaceful occupations and also on holiday jaunts. What a contrast from the Ypres Salient and the Arras area to such picturesque spots as Snapper Halt, Woody Bay, Parracombe and Lynton. The beauty of the scenery at these places must be seen to be believed, and to an old light railway man the journey itself adds a spice which completes the enjoyment.

A large amount of the track and rolling stock was bought and shipped to the Argentine, to be used in Agricultural development.

But for the difficulty of level crossings, the development of light railways would have been a paying proposition in this country, no doubt, as broad gauge extension is a costly undertaking, whilst the construction and operation of the light track is practically nothing in comparison.

What the light railway equipment cost would also make interesting reading. I was informed that a P.E. cost the Government £1,200. When one thinks of those P.E.s at Ashford and the many power units that had to be wrecked and abandoned during the British retirement in March, 1918, another aspect of the futility of war becomes evident.

Numerous former WDLR locomotives found new owners after the war including many of the Baldwin 4-6-0T. Amongst them was a pair regauged to 2ft 3³/₄ in gauge for the Snailbeach District Railway near Shrewsbury. Snailbeach No 4 (Baldwin 44572/17) poses for the camera at Callow Hill Quarry on May 5th, 1940.   *(Andrew Neale collection)*

List of Officers, NCOs and Men of the 31st Company

This list has been compiled from memory and in consequence is far from being complete; it may also be a little incorrect in one or two instances. The names and the ranks shown are mainly those who served during 1917, as so many changes took place after March, 1918, that it is difficult to recall them after that period.

Officers

Capt.	Burge, O.C., 1917		Capt.	Bean, O.C. 1918/19	
Lt.	Crewe		Lt.	Murry	Lt. Grant

NCOs and Men

Rank	Name	Role	Rank	Name	Role
C.Q.M.S.	Arnold	Control	Spr.	Craigan	Tinsmith
Spr.	Atkinson	Tract. Dr.	″	Crompton	Wagon Repairer
″	Addey	Cook			
Sgt.	Bell	Control	Cpl.	Disley	N.C.O. i/c Tract. Drs.
Spr.	Baker	Ord. Room			
″	Ball	Tract. Dr.	″	Davidson	N.C.O. i/c Guards
″	Barnett	″			
″	Bond	″	″	Denman	Tract. Repr. Shops
″	Bentley	″			
″	Bratt	″	″	Elam	N.C.O. i/c Canteen
″	Burchell	Guard (Wounded)	Spr.	Foy	P.E. Brakesman
			2/Cpl.	Goodenough	Tract. Dr.
2/Cpl.	Bullen	Carpenter			
Cpl.	Bulley	Storekeeper	Spr.	Guyer	Guard
″	Carpenter	Guard	Cpl.	Girvan	Camp Ord. Corp.
″	Cresswell	Timekeeper	C.Q.M.S.	Grainger	Control (Died 1929)
″	Crawford	Dist. Control			
″	Castle *Loco*	Repr. Shops	C.S.M.	Henderson	″
Spr.	Chennell	P.E. Tract. Dr.	Cpl.	Heritage	N.C.O. i/c Tract. Drs
″	Cartwright	Brakesman			
″	Cope	Loco Dr.	Spr.	Hughes	Tract. Dr.
2/Cpl.	Holmes	Tract. Dr.	2/Cpl.	Richards	Sub-control
Spr.	Hopwood	″	Spr.	Ryland	Tract. Shops
″	Hislop	Q.M.'s Stores	″	Restall	Sub-control
″	Hughes	Sub-control	″	Ruddick	P.E. Brakesman
2/Cpl.	Jennings	Dist. Control	Pnr.	Reardon	Camp Staff
″	Johnson	Camp Staff	R.Q.M.S.	Stace	
Cpl.	Jordan	Ord. Room	Sgt.	Storey	Dist. Control
Spr.	Kennedy	Tract. Rpr. Shops	″	Skelton	″
			″	Smalley	Tract. Shops (Died Dec 1919)

Spr.	Kite	Tract. Dr.			
R.S.M.	Lummis		Cpl.	Spence	Breakdown
Spr.	Lee	Tract. Dr.	Spr.	Sinclair	Cook
Sgt.	Leach	Shunter	”	Singleton	Tract. Dr.
Spr.	Muxworthy	Tract. Dr.	”	Sims	Stores
”	McKillip	Guard	”	Vanner	Tract. Dr.
”	Mullins	”	Sgt.	Williams	Tract. Repr. Shops
”	Musgrove	Shunter			
2/Cpl.	Mitchell	Tract. Dr.	”	Weare	Shunter
Spr.	Owen	Guard	”	Wells	Dist. Control
2/Cpl.	Ogilvie	Postman	Spr.	Walmsley	Loco Dr.
		(killed March 1919)	”	Walters	” (Uncle Sam)
Sgt.	Orrick	Breakdown			
C.S.M.	Pattinson	Ord. Room	”	Westwood	Guard
Cpl.	Pearce	Dist. Control	”	Wood	Tract. Dr.
Spr.	Poole	Tract. Dr.	Cpl.	Woods	Shunter
Sgt.	Rattray	Dist. Control	Spr.	York	Control
2/Cpl.	Randall	Tract. Dr.			

List of Officers, NCOs and Men of the 19th Company

Most of these names have been given by Mr W. Hill and also by the kind assistance of several members of the 19th who attended the 1933 Re-union.

Officers

Capt.	Barty	Capt.	Lovatt	Capt.	Thurburn
Lt.	Cannon	Lt.	Webster	Lt.	Allen
Lt.	Cooke *(killed)*	Lt.	Hire		

NCOs and Men

2/Cpl.	Allen	2/Cpl.	Dinnington
”	Ashcroft	Spr.	Downes
Spr.	Alderton	”	Day
C.Q.M.S.	Benson	Cpl.	Eaton
Cpl.	Bassington	Spr.	Edwards *(killed)*
2/Cpl.	Barton	”	Edmunds
L/Cpl.	Balls	”	Evans
Spr.	Blenkinsop	Cpl.	Flavell
”	Butcher	”	Fenwick *(killed)*
”	Beard	L/Cpl.	France
”	Beeston	Spr.	Franklin
”	Booth	R.S.M.	Gibbons
”	Baker	Sgt.	Goody
”	Brooks	Cpl.	Gibson
2/Cpl.	Chubb	2/Cpl.	Gower
”	Corrick	Spr.	Garner
Spr.	Coombs	”	Gover
”	Clowes	R.S.M.	Hamblin
”	Chown	C.Q.M.S.	Hutchinson
Cpl.	Davies	Cpl.	Hoppe
”	Difford	Spr.	Hill
Spr.	Hughes	L/Cpl.	Prendergast
”	Hardy	Spr.	Prickett
”	Harrington *(killed)*	”	Penton
”	Hoodless	”	Pryke
”	Hart *(died)*	”	Parr
”	Jenkins	Spr.	Roberts
”	Johnson	”	Rees
C.Q.M.S.	Kehler	”	Roberts
Cpl.	Kerr	Sgt.	Stimson
Sgt.	Long *(killed)*	Cpl.	Samuel
”	Lakey	2/Cpl.	Stiling

Spr.	Littler	"	Simcoe
Sgt.	Marshall *(killed)*	Spr.	Strutch
Cpl.	Murchie	"	Shipman
"	Moore	"	Saggars
"	Marritt	"	Stimson
"	Morton	"	Sargent
Spr.	McKay	Cpl.	Truman *(killed)*
"	Mayes	Spr.	Taylor *(killed)*
"	Macfarlane	"	V. Taylor
"	Maloney	2/Cpl.	Woodfine
C.Q.M.S.	Overton	"	Wingrove
Sgt.	Peake	Spr.	Williams
"	Prime	"	Williamson
Cpl.	Parker		

Appendix Four

Tractor Crews – Marcoing

The following is a Nominal Roll of the tractors and train crews comprising the 19th Company whilst stationed at Marcoing during the early part of 1919. It has been copied from a list kept as a souvenir by Mr W. Dunning who was NCO i/c of the train crews in those days.

NO.	DRIVER	GUARD	DRIVER	GUARD
P.E.				
1919	Singleton	Pinton	Griffiths	Tyers
1936	Holmes	Westwood	Mitchell	Dunsford
2006	Bratt	Hindle	Kitchen	Chappell
2016	Bayliss	-	Bridge	Haw
2061	Hunt	Stafford	Stewart	-
2062	Marley	Jamaiker	Coley	Staines
2077	Jackson	Hunt	Haines	McGeachy
40hp				
2317	Yates	Fletcher	Rhodes	Whyte
2295	Hopkinson	-	Bailey	-
2195	Coward	Pearce	Swan	Cavey
2277	Lewis	-	Adshead	-
2217	Wilde	Peakman	Hurst	Hewitson
2122	Frost	Chater	Preece	Phillips
3022	Shaw	Saunders	Luck	Chamberlain
2108	Clements	Burgess	Borrows	Rouse
2308	McCarthy	-	Corbin	-
3021	Manning	Restall	Kerrigan	McGrogan
3019	Hart	Jones	Longville	Sharp
2161	*Sent to Workshops*			
2279	Newton	Bryan	Trench	-
2221	Davies	-	O'Neill	-
2198	Blake	Ballantyne	Rose	-
20hp				
2385	Bishop	-	-	-
2459	Lister	-	-	-
2608	Goodyer	-	Thomas	-
70	Timms	-	-	-
2393	Blenkinsop	-	-	-

ON DUTY					OFF DUTY				
Loco Drivers	Firemen	Tractor Drivers	Brakesmen	Guards	Loco Drivers	Firemen	Tractor Drivers	Brakesmen	Guards
								Name	
				Name				"	
				"				"	
				"			Name	"	
		Name		"	Name	Name	"	"	Name
Name	Name	"	Name	"	"	"	"	"	"
"	"	"	"	"	"	"	"	"	"
"	"	"	"	"	Next for duty	Next for duty	Next for duty	Next for duty	Next for duty

Diagram of Duty Board installed in Timekeeper's Hut, referred to on page 18. The names were written on small blocks of wood which were placed in the appropriate slots as men booked on or off duty.

Diagram of Meal Indicator in Timekeeper's Hut, Orchard Camp, Arras

BREAKFAST	DINNER	TEA
• • • • • •	• • • • • • •	• • • • • • •
• • • • • •	• • • • • • •	• • • • • • •
• • • • • •	• • • • • • •	• • • • • • •
• • • • • •	• • • • • • •	• • • • • • •
	Nails for hanging discs with names inscribed	

Each N.C.O. and man applied to the Timekeeper for his disc before proceeding to the Mess Tent, where it was given up. The disc was afterwards replaced on the indicator in the section relating to the next meal by an Orderly. Thus a check was kept on the number of meals to be saved for those on duty, as referred to on page 19.